"In *Day-Votions for Mothers*, Rebecca Barlow Jordan takes us on a delightful, forty-day journey through the blessings and struggles of raising children. Her personal stories, told with humor and transparency, reveal the mother's heart within each of us, giving us a daily dose of hope and encouragement. Through thoughtful reflections, daily prayers, and examples of biblical moms, Jordan confirms our calling and celebrates the truth that we are not alone in the journey."

—Vonda Skelton, speaker and author of *Seeing through the Lies: Unmasking the Myths Women Believe*

"Rebecca gives sweet glimpses of motherhood, showing 'beauty in the midst,' while helping women see they aren't alone in common challenges. Through friendship and faith, Rebecca offers real-life choices and fresh perspective to energize mothers each day. I am excited about this Day-Votion™—it will encourage moms!"

—Judy Dippel, speaker and author of *Walking Through Postpartum Depression*

"This devotional brought me joy as well as a path to walk on daily with my Lord. Each day brought brand-new insights as Rebecca cleverly recapped the lesson with her Day-breaks and Day-briefs. This book will not leave my book table!"

—Lane P. Jordan, national speaker, singer, and author of *12 Steps to Becoming a More Organized Mom*

"Rebecca understands the emotional, physical, and spiritual exhaustion of motherhood. She also knows the secret to refreshing, refueling, and renewing a mother's soul. Like a trusted friend, Rebecca takes you by the hand and leads you to God's still waters for the encouragement you need to meet the day's demands. You'll walk away filled to the brim and ready to pour into your children's lives anew."

—Sharon Jaynes, international conference speaker and author of *Being a Great Mom, Raising Great Kids and Becoming the Woman of His Dreams*

DAY-VOTIONS®
for mothers

*Heart to Heart
Encouragement*

Rebecca Barlow Jordan

ZONDERVAN®

ZONDERVAN.com/
AUTHORTRACKER
follow your favorite authors

ZONDERVAN

Day-votions® for Mothers
Copyright © 2010 by Rebecca Barlow Jordan

This title is also available as a Zondervan ebook.
Visit www.zondervan.com/ebooks.

This title is also available in a Zondervan audio edition.
Visit www.zondervan.fm.

Requests for information should be addressed to:

Zondervan, *Grand Rapids, Michigan 49530*

Library of Congress Cataloging-in-Publication Data

Jordan, Rebecca.
    Day-votions for mothers : heart-to-heart encouragement /
  Rebecca Barlow Jordan.
      p. cm.
    ISBN 978-0-310-32204-7 (hardcover, jacketed)
    1. Mothers—Prayers and devotions. 2. Christian women—Prayers and
  devotions I. Title.
  BV4847.J685—2009
  242'.6431—dc22   2009040173

Interior design: Michelle Espinoza

Printed in the United States of America

---

11 12 13 14 15 16 /DCI/ 22 21 20 19 18 17 16 15 14 13 12 11 10 9 8 7 6 5 4

To Valerie and Jennifer,
who make being a mom both a joy and a treasure

contents

Special Thanks / 11
Encouragement for Mothers / 14
Poem / 16

Day 1 — Too Little Resting, Too Little Nesting / 17
Day 2 — New Beginnings / 20
Day 3 — Stone Memorials / 24
Day 4 — Mom in the Middle / 27
Day 5 — The Letter / 31
Day 6 — Listen and Learn / 34
Day 7 — Passin' It On / 37
Day 8 — Written in Stone / 40
Day 9 — De-feathering the Nest / 44
Day 10 — The Best Gift of All / 48
Day 11 — Play Dates and Pray Dates / 51
Day 12 — Cut the Cord! / 56
Day 13 — Sleepless in the Battle / 59
Day 14 — Truth or Consequences / 63
Day 15 — Their Day Will Come / 67
Day 16 — Spiritual Myopia / 71
Day 17 — Taming the Untamable / 74

Day 18 — This Too Shall Pass / 78

Day 19 — Small Offerings, Big Rewards / 82

Day 20 — It Takes So Little / 86

Day 21 — Sex after Kids? / 89

Day 22 — One Day at a Time / 94

Day 23 — Always in School / 97

Day 24 — Investments for Life / 100

Day 25 — Creative Legacies / 104

Day 26 — Knee Prints / 107

Day 27 — Extravagant Love / 112

Day 28 — True Greatness / 116

Day 29 — The Great Escape / 120

Day 30 — Behind Closed Doors / 123

Day 31 — Desperate Moms / 127

Day 32 — Forever Flowers / 131

Day 33 — Pause to Refresh / 135

Day 34 — The Friendship Connection / 139

Day 35 — The Real Model / 143

Day 36 — King's Kids / 147

Day 37 — When the New Mom Comes to Town / 151

Day 38 — A Higher Calling / 155

Day 39 — Switched at Birth / 160

Day 40 — Beauty in the Midst / 164

Epilogue / 169

Notes / 171

special thanks

In writing a book of encouragement for others, I must thank those who have encouraged me in the process. So many have had a part.

I'm so thankful for a great editor like Sue Brower who has been like a cheerleader — patiently encouraging, listening, answering questions, and believing in my writing. Her enthusiasm about this project from day one has filled me with an even greater passion to write my heart. You're the best, Sue! Thanks also to freelance editor Lori VandenBosch for her editing and encouraging comments, and to Verlyn Verbrugge for his editing skills. Thanks to marketing director Karwyn Bursma and her extremely talented team for their beautiful work on the book's cover and creativity in their marketing.

I appreciate Joyce Ondersma and Jackie Aldridge in author relations and the wonderful Zondervan sales team. And to the entire Zondervan staff, including support team, for your willingness to publish this project. How can I say thank you enough for all you do? This book would not be possible without all of you at Zondervan.

A special thanks to Steve Laube, for his integrity and diligence as my agent and friend. His invaluable background and knowledge of the writing business have given superb direction to my writing. I so appreciate his encouragement and patience, his belief in my gifts, and his ability to find a home for my writing dreams so quickly. Thank you, Steve, for your enthusiasm for this new Day-votions series.

Thanks to my friend Karen-Atkins Milton who gave generously of her time to look over many of these day-votions and offer another woman's perspective. To those who prayed for me throughout the writing of this book: my precious daughters and sons-in law, Valerie, Jennifer, Shawn, and Craig, who also allowed me to share their stories, other family members, friends, church members, my Bible study class, and the women of my personal, prayer support team: Priscilla Adams, Mary Griffin, Ruth Inman, Sharon Hogan, and Kim Coffman — your prayers and encouragement made such a difference. Thanks also to those moms and friends who shared transparent examples from their lives in this book, which will no doubt encourage many in their walk with the Lord.

I appreciate Warner Press for allowing me to use some bulletin copy I wrote for them and DaySpring for letting me use some of the greeting card copy they previously published for me.

There is no way to adequately thank my precious husband for his prayers, support, and encouragement. Larry not only blessed me by offering his thorough editing skills and great communication abilities in reading through every day-votion. He gave up his own comfort and rare personal time, taking over many of my everyday tasks to do whatever was necessary to help me complete this manuscript. With his love, integrity, and unselfishness he has influenced this writing more than anyone else, so that together, we could be a team in ministry. I could not write without his loving support. I love you, Larry! You are one of God's greatest blessings to me!

And to my precious heavenly Father and Lord Jesus, there will never be enough words to adequately praise you for who you are. Nor could I ever count the times you have continually blessed me in ways I could never deserve. For every time I cry, "I can't!" you always answer, "But I can!" You, Lord, are the passion of my heart. You are the One who encourages me daily, who satisfies my soul hunger, and who fills me with purpose. Thank you for allowing me the joy of writing about you and the privilege of sharing encouragement with others.

encouragement for mothers

Motherhood is indeed a divine calling. Mothers come in all shapes and sizes, but God stamps "original" on each of our lives. Our needs vary. Sometimes we don't even know what those are. Overstressed and in need of rest, we search for quiet places to restore and regroup. Yet feeling isolated and alone, we crave understanding and companionship — other moms, friends, and family members who will share our load and celebrate our joys.

And though we are unique individuals, every mother needs — and wants — encouragement and deeper, more meaningful relationships with her children, family, God, and others.

For years I've tried to write devotions that would encourage readers to connect on a deeper, more intimate level with God and others: to "love the Lord your God with all your heart and with all your soul and with all your strength and with all your mind" and to "love your neighbor as yourself" (Luke 10:27).

But sometimes "life" happens, and we moms forget how to do that. We realize that love hurts and relationships take work. Parenting zaps our energy, hearts are broken, and our minds get confused. We forget what we were made for, and we forget how much God truly loves us. Yet the longing for connection lingers, like the fragrance in a home when a sweet candle's flame has been extinguished.

I could offer you a few motivational thoughts to lift your spirits temporarily, but they would not satisfy your heart hunger for long. In this new series of Day-votions®, I've tried to say to you as mothers, "You are not alone." None of us is. Our very existence depends on strong relationships. In bite-sized, *day-votions* for everyday living, I've written some nuggets of spiritual encouragement that I hope will help you strengthen your relationship with God, with your children, and with others. I pray these stories, insights, and biblical truths will direct you to the only One who can meet all of your needs. As you draw close to Jesus, I believe he will connect the dots to more meaningful relationships with others as well.

Whether you're dealing with finances, parenting, inadequacy, or guilt, you're not alone in your struggles and challenges. Other women have — and are — walking the same path as you. It doesn't matter if you're a single mom, married, young, middle-aged, or a senior, God is by your side, applauding your work, extending fresh hope, and drawing you close to himself so he can whisper, "You *are* making a difference. I'm here to help you, and I will take care of you. I love you. I always will."

Through these pages, I hope you'll laugh a little and maybe cry a little, but more than anything, my heart's desire is that you will be encouraged to keep on loving, laughing, serving, and sharing — and that you will gain a new sense of joy and purpose in this beautiful God-ordained role of being a mother.

"May our Lord Jesus himself and God our Father, who loved us and by his grace gave us eternal encouragement and good hope, encourage your hearts and strengthen you in every good deed and word" (2 Thessalonians 2:16 – 17).

Rebecca

God (Jesus) hears the cries of a mother's heart —
He is her Heavenly Father.
God celebrates the joys of a mother's heart —
He is her King of Kings.
God nurtures the wounds of a mother's heart —
He is her Great Physician.
God meets the needs of a mother's heart —
He is her Good Shepherd.
God sees the compassion of a mother's heart —
He is her Wonderful Counselor.
God places the love in a mother's heart —
He is her Awesome Creator.[1]

- RBJ

day 1

too little resting,
too little nesting

It's useless to rise early and go to bed late,
and work your worried fingers to the bone.
Don't you know he enjoys giving rest to those he loves?
Psalm 127:2 (MSG)

What mom hasn't uttered the words "Hurry up!" to her children? From toddlers to teens, my children heard those words fly out of my mouth far too many times. Were they poking or primping? Was it my time management? Or my kids'? My own expectations? Or others'? Regardless of the cause, the days seemed to shrink as the hours clicked by far too quickly.

I know I'm not alone. Is there too much "hurry" in your life? Too much pursuing and too much doing? Too little resting and too little nesting? The executive mom, driven by the demands in her office, exceeds the "need" limit continually. The young mother juggles frantically her sixty-hour workload to make ends meet. Husband and wife wring their hands and arrest their hearts in exhaustion.

Is there another way? God says there is. Tired bodies cannot function on high-speed frenzy forever. Obviously, we cannot turn back the clock. Time never stands still, and we all face similar struggles. Others need you, whether it's your children, husband, employer, neighbor, or friend. But sooner or later, something has to give. Moms have needs too.

There is no "one-size-fits-all" time solution for mothers. Children's needs are uniquely different, and trying to nourish their spiritual, emotional, and physical needs require resources beyond our control. Then add everything else we as moms try to juggle. Is there a boundary line? How do you say, "Enough"? Even sleep eludes us, and we find our minds racing through the night, desperate for solutions to our dilemma.

> *God will give every mom the resources she needs*
> *to accomplish what he wants for her to do.*

I remind my daughters often that some things will change through the years, that sleepless nights of feeding, changing, rocking, and crying will pass away (do I hear an *amen?*). But even as the kids grow, we as moms can always find activities to fill the gaps and accompanying worries to zap our energy in the process. If we make a habit — and a lifestyle — of hurrying and worrying, everyone loses.

God will give every mom the resources she needs to accomplish what he wants for her to do. In the meantime, he says our overscheduled, undernourished lives get us nowhere — nowhere near to his ideal for us. Even as we sleep, cannot God who knows us inside out produce wisdom, rest, creativity, and solutions if we rest in his provision, not our own?

If we work for anything, let it be that we work to nest — in his rest.

DAY-BREAK

Think through a typical day's activities. What things can you subtract? Any priorities you should add? See how many times you can eliminate the word "Hurry!" this week.

DAY-BRIEF

Wrestle less; trust more.

DAY-VOTEDLY YOURS

Lord, forgive me when I try to cram too many hours into one day. Thank you for reminding me that as I rest in you, my children will sense my refreshed spirit as well.

day 2
new beginnings

I prayed for this child, and the LORD has granted me
what I asked of him. So now I give him to the LORD.
For his whole life he will be given over to the LORD.
1 Samuel 1:27 – 28

For months I visualized the scene. How would I deal with my child's reluctance to enter kindergarten? What would I say to her as she held on to my pants leg with terror in her eyes? What would I do when she started screaming, "No, Mom, don't make me go to school! I don't want to go! What will I do without you?"

Well, the big day finally arrived. Just as I envisioned, we walked the short distance to school hand-in-hand. My toddler ambled along beside us, ready to join in the adventure. As we stood in front of the classroom doors, I looked at my daughter and said, "It's time, honey." I held my breath and then watched as my five-year-old grinned and eagerly sprinted toward the door.

"Wait!" I cried, clinging to her hand. "Don't go! Don't go! What's Mom going to do without you?"

Well, it didn't happen exactly like that. But you get the picture. Depending on your child's personality — and ours — sometimes letting go is easier for our kids than for us as moms. You may have left them in others' care many times, but kindergarten is the first step toward, *gulp*, moving them out of your nest. Those who opt for Christian home schooling may feel more secure, but the fact still remains: your child is growing up.

Questions march across the screen of your imagination like fearful soldiers: Will my child be safe, loved, accepted? Will she find friends? Will he encounter enough Christian influence? Will God take care of him? Will she learn the right things?

Another woman faced the same dilemma. God finally blessed a barren woman named Hannah with a handsome baby boy. She nurtured him until the day came when she knew it was time to let go. Fulfilling a previous promise to God, Hannah deposited her young son, Samuel, into the hands of a priest named Eli. There at the temple, Samuel would serve as Eli's assistant. Eli would raise this dedicated young man to be a servant of God.

Can you imagine the fears of this young mother as she let go of her firstborn's hand and waved a tearful goodbye? Was Eli trustworthy? Would Samuel be safe, loved, accepted? Would God take care of him?

> *Hannah did not give her son to Eli;*
> *she gave him into the hands of the Lord.*

The Bible doesn't mention Hannah's fears, but it does record her trust. Read it for yourself:

"My heart rejoices in the Lord; in the Lord my horn is lifted high. My mouth boasts over my enemies, for I delight in your deliverance. There is no one holy like the Lord; there is no one besides you; there is no Rock like our God" (1 Samuel 2:1 – 2).

How could she feel this way? Hannah did not give her son to Eli; she gave him into the hands of the Lord.

What about her son's reactions? Hannah returned home with her husband, but 1 Samuel 2:11 says Samuel thrived: "the boy ministered before the LORD under Eli the priest." Hannah's decision to "let go" and trust God with her child resulted in a new spokesman for a nation named Israel, as God raised up the great prophet Samuel.

Since kindergarten, I had to "let go" many times as my children passed one milestone after another: first day at middle school and high school, first boyfriend and subsequent dating, first day of driving, first day of college, then graduation.

I pleaded for protection; I probed for wisdom; I prepared for the worst; I prayed for the best. Fears still nipped at my heels with every new stage, but God's faithfulness filled me with a growing trust as the years flew by. I didn't always usher my children into their exciting adventures with joyful anticipation like Hannah, but by the time the big wedding day arrived, I had learned how to celebrate.

As we walked through the doors of our home after waving good-bye to our daughter and her new husband, I looked my husband in the eye and said, "Honey, let's party!"

Even God had to "let go" of his own Son. And because he did, Jesus' death and resurrection resulted in a new beginning for us. Our whole future changed. And we have all of eternity to celebrate.

DAY-BREAK

What new beginnings are you celebrating with your child/children? Examine your trust level. How hard is it for you to let go of your own kids and release them into God's hands?

DAY-BRIEF

Letting go is always easier when we add just one letter: Go-*d*.

DAY-VOTEDLY YOURS

Lord, I know you love my children even more than I do. Forgive me when I cling to fear instead of to your faithful hand. I give my children to you, for the only truly safe place for them to be is in Jesus.

day 3
stone memorials

*In the future, when your children ask you, "What do
these stones mean?" tell them that the flow of the Jordan
was cut off before the ark of the covenant of the LORD ...
These stones are to be a memorial to the people of Israel forever.*
Joshua 4:6 – 7

Family stories. Don't you love them? Tales of quirky relatives bring
a smile to our lips, while revealed secrets evoke embarrassed sighs.
What exactly do our children need to hear and remember? God
says our legacy should include sharing not only those exciting
moments in biblical history when God showed up, but also those
experiences when God created a path for us personally. Our children need to hear how the awesome presence of God made the difference between death and life, and how he has touched our lives,
even in ordinary ways. Those stories are the "stones" of our faith,
the personal proof in our lives that says, "God is faithful! God is
good! God is victorious!"

Embedded in my children's hearts are memories: spectacular
moments in the mountains of Colorado, seaside adventures on the
California beaches, and fun family times, both in a desert cabin
and snow-tubing down the slopes in Arizona. But if you ask them
what they remember most, they will most likely tell you about the
amazing times God showed up. How could they forget the vacation

when we made a wrong turn? Our car died — in the middle of nowhere, but down the highway from a tiny farmhouse — where a car repairman named Juan just happened to live.

How could they fail to remember God's miraculous provision, when, after searching all over the town of Farmington, New Mexico, for a needed car part, Juan discovered the exact piece hanging on the wall of his garage workshop — that just happened to fit our car? And none of us will ever forget the restoration God brought to Juan's formerly hardened heart that day, or the angelic glow that hovered over his head as he and his family joined hands with ours in a prayer of blessing and thanksgiving.

We had planned to cross over the nearby mountain pass that day, but God amended our plans. The wrong turn was a right one, after all. We discovered the next day when we arrived at our destination, that had we crossed without God's intervention, we would have found no lodging. Everything was full. Memories like those are permanent stones — and we rehearse them often.

If our children are not asking, "What do these stones mean?" it's not God's fault.

If our children are not asking, "What do these stones mean?" it's not God's fault. The same God who dammed the waters of the Jordan River so his people could cross is the same God who waits to act on our behalf today. He created each mom uniquely, so we can have special stories of our own to tell our children. The special bond between mom and child will grow through the sharing of those memories together. As you rehearse those experiences, those stones will line a path for your children toward a deeper relationship with God.

You may be thinking, *But all I can remember are small stones — no earth-shattering, miraculous moments.* It doesn't matter. Mountains are often built one pebble at a time. Build memorials between the mountains of laundry, the concrete highways, and the stony foundations of your home. God is working everywhere.

Are there still immoveable stones in your life? Let your children pray with you even about those stones — so together, when the answer comes, you can all "cross over" and celebrate the stories of God's faithfulness with the new stones of remembrance God has given you.

DAY-BREAK

Think back over your life. Do you see any "stones" there? Step over the stones of regret. Or better yet, when age-appropriate, share the lessons God taught you from your "stumbling stones." What impossible stones has God moved for you? How has he built your faith or answered your prayers?

DAY-BRIEF

Some stones break bones. Others build bridges.

DAY-VOTEDLY YOURS

Father, forgive me when I suffer from spiritual amnesia. Thank you for all the times you have blessed me in the past. Help me share those times with my children and to recognize future opportunities to build new stones.

day 4
mom in the middle

LORD, you understand; remember me and care for me.
Jeremiah 15:15

My mom lived only five weeks after she was diagnosed with cancer. My brother and his wife, who lived nearby, brought Mom into their home during those last weeks, and hospice care was wonderful. However, none of us really thought Mother would die so soon.

I had visited Mom twice earlier with my sister, in about a two-month period. The second time my mother had a seizure, forcing her to the hospital to find out the reason for that as well as her progressing weak condition. We never expected the diagnosis that came.

After hearing the doctor's report, I had to return home a few days later, a day's drive away. I planned to return and see Mom before Christmas, knowing her time could be short, but a week after I arrived home, my husband had some back spasms that sent him to the floor and into bed for over two weeks. My children were flying in for Christmas soon, so we only had a few days' opening in which to go back and see Mom. When that time came, my husband's back was not yet healed. So we couldn't go. I didn't want to leave him. I felt torn as a mom in the middle. I wanted to be there with my mother, but I was also needed to minister to my own family.

I prayed fervently, "Lord, please let me see Mother one more time before she dies. If possible, I want to be there when that happens." But the call came too early. Mother died two days before Christmas.

Whatever the situation, God knows your limitations.

I wept and grieved, but knew God had answered another larger prayer we had all been asking — for Mother not to suffer long, and for her to die peacefully. I was so grateful for that and knew Mom was already enjoying a reunion in heaven with loved ones and the Lord himself. But I was plagued with guilt-ridden thoughts: *Why didn't God let me go? Loved ones are supposed to gather around their family members in their last moments. I talked with Mom by phone only a few days before her death. I told her I loved her. She told me the same. But what did she really think? Did she think I abandoned her? Did she think I didn't care? Did she know I really wanted to be there? I should have been there for her.*

After Mom's death, God eased my pain in many ways. Even at the funeral God reminded me of a story Mom had written (we found it only weeks before she died) of how God protected her when she was caught in the middle of a dangerous thunderstorm and assured her she would never be alone. He would always be with her.

Then later as I was sifting through some of Mom's things, I uncovered a cache of letters from my own grandmother, written to Mother during my grandmother's serious illness. "Don't worry about coming," my grandmother had said. "I am fine, and others are looking after me." I read between the lines the unspoken words, "I'm not alone."

That was written shortly before my grandmother's death. My mom had just moved to another state for a new ministry with my dad, far away from her own mother. Her mom died before she could make the trip back. Then it hit me. My mom was a pastor's wife like me. *She must have felt the same way I do,* I thought. *She wanted to be there for her mom, but circumstances prevented her from coming until the funeral too. She knew what it was like to be helplessly caught in the middle.*

At times you may feel like the filling of an Oreo cookie. Sandwiched between two generations, you can't be in two places at once. Your family needs you; your aging mom needs you. You may feel squeezed between in-laws and your own parents, or between your birth children and stepchildren. Whatever the situation, God knows your limitations — and he doesn't place unreal expectations on you. Hopefully, your family won't either.

But even if they do, you can rest in the assurance that you are never alone. Jesus stands in the middle, ready to help. He *can* be in all places at once, even when we can't. He alone understands, and that's all that really matters.

DAY-BREAK

Have you ever felt like a mom in the middle? How did you handle the situation? What would you do differently in the future?

DAY-BRIEF

The best thing about Jesus being our mediator is that he never takes sides. He only takes control.

DAY-VOTEDLY YOURS

Jesus, I'm so weary at times of trying to meet all the needs around me. I can't do it! But I know you can. Thank you for understanding. Please take over when I feel squeezed in impossible situations. Lord, I trust you!

day 5
the letter

I have loved you with an everlasting love.
Jeremiah 31:3

When my children were small, I began a ritual that rolled around twice a year, once for each daughter. I had grown up with simple family birthday celebrations. I can only remember a couple of actual birthday "parties." Even though I tried to plan more for my own daughters, like an occasional piñata party or teddy bear birthday cake, we often ended up with simple family times as well.

I'm sure they would have loved bigger and better celebrations. Now their own children's parties feature yearly themes, creative birthday cakes, and sometimes bounce houses bulging with giggling friends and classmates.

But I did what I could do best. On a limited budget, instead of planning large parties, I penned simple words. I called it "The Birthday Letter." I missed the first few years but began writing them about the time they started elementary school. In the first letter I expressed a mom's delight in seeing them the very first time they were born, describing all the emotions and celebrations of their arrivals. I emphasized what a wonderful gift they were from God, how much they were growing, and how much I loved them. On special years or events, like age thirteen, sixteen, and on graduation, my husband and I both wrote letters. But selfishly, I volunteered for most of them.

I visualized God's dreams for them and told them how much they reflected Jesus more each year. On milestone years I celebrated their successes and included generous splashes of homespun wisdom as well as simple spiritual truths. At first, the letters fit on one page. But the older they grew, the faster my pen wrote — and the more emotions burst from my sentimental mother's heart.

I'm glad the girls have expressed the desire to keep those letters accumulated through the years. Hopefully some day after we're gone, they will read those words and remember — at just the time they need them: a word of encouragement, a whisper of pride, a shout of joy from a mother's heart, penned with tears and a heart full of love.

Today emails, text messages, and cell phone calls have replaced the medium of snail mail letters. After all, paper takes space — and trees — and most of all, time. But there's something about a handwritten letter that says, "I love you. I care about you. You're special. And you're worth the time and effort."

The message is so clear that no child could ever doubt his intentions or his love.

God wrote a letter to his children. He called it the Bible. Throughout this volume of heaven-breathed words he scattered affirmations visualizing his dreams for us: "The plans I have for you ... to give you hope" (Jeremiah 29:11); wise instructions to ensure our success: "The fear of the LORD is the beginning of knowledge" (Proverbs 1:7); and personal promises to meet our every need: "I will never leave you nor forsake you" (Joshua 1:5).

His letters are so important that they've been preserved through the years. And the message is so clear that no child could ever doubt his intentions or his love.

The most amazing thing is that even though they were written for everyone ("For God so loved the world," John 3:16), each time I read those letters, I find a word of encouragement, a whisper of pride, and a shout of joy from his heart, personalized with tears from his heart to mine.

It is a keepsake that will endure for all time.

DAY-BREAK

Have you ever written a letter to your children? No matter what age they are, write them a birthday letter this year. Include all the special qualities that make them unique. Let your children know how proud you are of them and that you will always love them.

DAY-BRIEF

The best things are said with the heart — and a pen — again and again.

DAY-VOTEDLY YOURS

Lord, thank you for giving me your special letter of all time — and for all the love it represents. Form the words in my heart so I can express to my own children how much they mean to me. Help me to never let a day go by without telling them I love them.

listen and learn

But we were gentle among you,
like a mother caring for her little children.
1 Thessalonians 2:7 (NIV)

"You went to that conference but didn't change a bit!"

I couldn't believe the words from my preschooler's mouth. I had explained to her earlier that Mom and Dad were attending a meeting that would help us be better parents. I guess I thought my truthfulness would ward off any separation anxiety. But frustration got the best of me when I walked through the door and discovered my children still up late that night after the conference. Apparently they had tested the babysitter and won the battle of wills.

Instead of responding appropriately with firmness and gentleness, I overreacted, and my preschooler's expectations of a changed parent vanished. What about *my* expectations? Hadn't she let *me* down?

Chip Ingram says, "So much of our lack of patience is simply pride rooted in our failure to accept that we don't need others' approval and we don't need to prove ourselves superior."[2]

Hmm. Most of the time I was pretty easy-going. But I thought about the times when I demonstrated a lack of patience. Poor sleep, physical ailments, or unusual stress goaded me, like all young moms, into less-than-gentle moods on occasion. In these instances, it didn't take much to send both my children and me over the edge.

All moms occasionally experience challenges to their motherly authority that may light a temporary short fuse. In those moments, gentleness is often absent. Why?

For me, the answer comes in a divine whisper in my spirit. *Pride.* Pride? Does anger make me feel superior to my kids? Is that the fuel that feeds my impatient spirit at times?

Why would Paul use a mother's interaction between herself and her children as an analogy and example of how he had treated his fellow believers? Because gentleness is power under control. Gentleness is not a stick of dynamite with a short or long fuse. It is an explosive, powerful training tool with no fuse at all. When we allow the Holy Spirit to be in control, he will replace the fuse and remove the need to *prove* anything. Anger begets anger. Others — especially children — usually respond to gentleness.

Sometimes God lets our children be the teachers.

My preschool daughter's accusation did more to change my expectations and outer reactions than any conference. In the future, I would still discipline disobedience, but with a different attitude. As I changed — guess what? — so did my children. And when we both blew it, sincere apologies, hugs, and kisses quickly followed.

Our children are just kids, not little adults. They haven't mastered the art of patience. Neither have we as moms. But we are the nurturers. We are the ones to lead by example. Children often mimic what they see and hear.

Sometimes God lets our children be the teachers. At those times, we would be wise to listen — and learn.

DAY-BREAK

When are you most tempted to be angry with your child? How would you like to respond? Write down what you will do the next time your child challenges your limits.

DAY-BRIEF

Gentleness is dynamite with the fuse removed.

DAY-VOTEDLY YOURS

Lord, forgive me when I allow pride to dictate my actions and reactions. You are the Blessed Controller of my life. Make gentleness the rule of my actions, so my children can feel accepted, loved, and secure.

day 7
passin' it on

*Do not forget the things your eyes have seen or let them
slip from your heart as long as you live. Teach them
to your children and to their children after them.*
Deuteronomy 4:9

As I approached the end of a lesson on wisdom, I challenged my Bible study class to list some things they learned — or were learning — about life. I encouraged them to share one or two in class. Then in an email follow-up, I suggested they write a letter to their children, expressing their love and some of the things they had learned in life so far on their journey. Some had teenagers; others' children were in college; and one still had an elementary-age child at home.

"I've learned that God does not limit the number of miracles a person can have," offered one mom who had survived three bouts of cancer.

Another mom spoke up. "I've learned never to say never."

Still another added, "My clock is not God's clock."

Our children have probably memorized our age-old "momisms" and the lessons we moms try to teach them, because we verbalize them so often: "Always treat others as you want to be treated." "Love sometimes hurts." "Don't count your chickens before they hatch." "This too shall pass."

Just before President George W. Bush left office, I read some quotes from his speech to some 3,700 Texas A&M graduates and 6,300 guests: "Remember that popularity is as fleeting as the Texas wind. Character and conscience are as sturdy as the oaks on this campus." Later he added, "Listen to your mother. She's still telling me what to do."[3]

And then there are some truths that your children are learning without your saying a word — and you don't even realize it. Those are the keepers.

Not long ago on our fortieth wedding anniversary, our daughters gave us a beautiful scrapbook filled with photos, cards, letters, and memories from both friends and family. We laughed, cried, and reminisced as we turned the pages of our lives represented in that special gift.

A mother knows her own inadequacies and fears and the mistakes she made known only to her and God. Her fears run deep that her children might repeat her failures and inherit her faults. Often our minds replay the negative messages and hide the positive ones. *Have I taught them enough? What lessons have they learned? What kind of legacy am I leaving them?* God wants us to focus on the good memories and positive lessons.

God wants us to focus on the good memories and positive lessons.

If the truth were known, perhaps the majority of things (good or bad) our kids learn are lessons that are "caught," not "taught." I discovered within those scrapbook pages that my kids have forgiving hearts. Apparently they learned that "love covers over all wrongs" (Proverbs 10:12), because they neglected to mention our mistakes, instead listing things we taught them that we never remembered saying verbally.

We never hid our shortcomings from our children. At the appropriate time, we hung them out in the open like damp clothes on an old-fashioned clothesline. With great care and tenderness, God dried them, along with the tears we all shed together.

Within those scrapbook pages I saw a reflection of God's grace and goodness in the penned words of my own daughters. I could list many lessons I've learned in life. But *they've* taught *me* one of the most important ones:

"Children are precious."

DAY-BREAK

Take time to write down at least three important lessons you've learned in life so far. Then share them with your children. If your children are still at home, give each of them a special hug today and tell them how glad you are they belong to you.

DAY-BRIEF

Your children are often the mirrors of your life.

DAY-VOTEDLY YOURS

Lord, teach us your truths so we can pass them on to our children. Fill the pages of our lives with scraps of love, grace, and goodness — all the rich blessings you instilled in us as moms. Thank you for the privilege of being a mother.

written in stone

Do not move an ancient boundary stone set up by your ancestors.
Proverbs 22:28

Linda and her college-age son, Kevin, who was home on spring break, were in an intense discussion about the Bible's relevance. "Everyone knows the Ten Commandments are outdated pieces of stone," said Kevin.

"Oh? Where are you getting your information?"

"None of my friends believe or practice them. And my history professor says those rules are too harsh and don't work anymore. He calls them intolerant."

Linda started to argue, then thought better. "What do you think, Kevin?"

Kevin averted his eyes. "I'm ... not sure anymore."

"Would you like to talk about it later?"

You may never experience that kind of conversation with your children, but chances are you will hear some challenges and possibly some accusations. Some of you may be labeled "old fashioned" or "out of touch."

Against the backdrop of a postmodern culture, our kids hear every philosophy and argument imaginable. We can't prevent or protect them from everything harmful. But may I encourage you as a mom, especially if you are raising young children, to stand firm and keep the "ancient boundary lines" intact?

In the Bible, the ancient boundary line determined the physical border of a person's land, marked off by stones. The law was clear. Anyone moving those stones would be charged with stealing land.[4]

Sound rules, like God's laws, show us the clear-cut lines between right and wrong.

God sets boundaries for a reason. He has created us and knows our sinful tendencies. That's why he gave us laws like the Ten Commandments. They won't save us. Only Jesus' death and resurrection provide salvation. But they give us boundaries to protect others and ourselves — and to show us our wrong behavior and its consequences. They offer basic principles for life. In essence, from the beginning of time, even in the Garden of Eden, God loved us too much to give us freedom without boundaries.

If you are a mom who has moved the "ancient boundary stones" with your kids, you may not consider it mistreatment, much less "stealing." You may rationalize it as self-preservation. What mom doesn't suffer battle fatigue sometimes? What mom hasn't felt pinned to the wall by a firing squad of young rebels, all taking aim at her simultaneously? But in the long run, aren't you doing your child an injustice? Sound rules, like God's laws, are for our best interest and protection. They show us the clear-cut lines between right and wrong. And they demonstrate that you love your kids too much to give them freedom without boundaries.

"But what about grace?" you may argue. "Shouldn't we bend the rules at times?" Grace is not necessarily about bending rules, nor is it not ignoring or shrinking what is right. Grace may amend the punishment, choosing not to give us what we deserve. But grace also means the power to *do* what is right — for you and your child. And ancient doesn't always mean old.

When it comes to boundaries, *ancient* means sound — and wise. Guard the "ancient boundaries," not as harsh judges without mercy, but as loving caretakers of God's children on loan to you. Keep standing for right, even if your kids sometimes choose wrong (and they will). God will give you wisdom, and your children will love and respect you for it (even if they won't admit it).

What about when they question you? Let God's grace guide you, but don't be afraid to tell them, "Some things are written in stone."

DAY-BREAK

At what times are you most tempted to give in and "move the ancient boundaries" — the clear-cut rules you have in place? Do your children know without a doubt what those boundaries are? Are the consequences dispensed with grace?

DAY-BRIEF

The law of love supersedes all others.

DAY-VOTEDLY YOURS

Lord, when I'm battle weary and a little teary, I'll be on my knees. You are the only one who gives me strength to hold the line. Help me remember, my children are not enemies; they are gifts from you. Teach me how to parent with firmness and grace.

de-feathering the nest

[He guarded him] like an eagle that stirs up its nest
and hovers over its young,
that spreads its wings to catch them
and carries them aloft.

Deuteronomy 32:11

Kenneth Price shares a beautiful comparison of the Golden Eagle with a Christian's life in his book *The Eagle Christian*.[5] The male and female eagle literally lock their talons and flip head over heels in love as they seal their marriage ceremony. They then begin the business of building a nest, a virtual fortress for their future eaglets.

The father eagle completes the building of the outside nest with large limbs and branches on the cleft of a rock, sometimes as high as ten thousand feet. The mother eagle soon settles down into the nest to cushion a sweet home, gathering leaves, grass, and other soft treasures to decorate and pad the nest.

Just before the baby eaglets hatch, Mother Eagle begins to do a curious thing. She starts plucking some of the downy soft feathers from her breast and smoothes them like a carpet over the floor of the nest. She does this so that the sharp branches and twigs don't poke and stick the babies.

Life continues and the eaglets begin to grow. One day the mama starts pecking away at the soft, velvety carpet and then grabs up hunks with her powerful talons. She doesn't want them to become too comfortable. She knows they must learn to stand on their own without her feathery protection. All of a sudden, the kids start squirming and hollering, "Ouch! Mom, those branches are hurting us!"

Then one day, Mama Eagle starts acting very strange. She starts stirring up the nest, and her powerful, six- to ten-foot span reaches all the way across the nest. She may start pushing her "teen" eaglets gently — then harder and more directly. They cringe at the edge of the nest, mortified. At times she may even hover over the nest, dangling food, enticing them closer to the edge.

We moms are not on this child-raising journey alone.

One morning Mom wakes up with that *look* in her eyes. The kids cower and whisper to one another. "Look out! Mom's on the warpath!"

And then it happens — a kid's scariest nightmare — and the worst case of PMS they've ever seen in their mom. Mama Eagle stirs a little too hard, and those eaglets go flying over the edge of the nest.

Only they're not flying — they're flailing those wings as panic fills their eyes. "We're gonna diiiie!" they yell in unison as they plunge toward the ground.

But up above them a tiny figure is circling round and round. The eaglets see nothing but their early graves down below. Just before the eaglets hit the hard earth, Father or Mother Eagle, who can see from miles away and can fly vertically over two hundred miles per hour, comes streaking down in the nick of time. Huge, strong wings dip and scoop up the eaglets just before they crash land.

The parents will repeat this cycle, until one day the eaglets are falling for the last time. Their parent-child game suddenly turns into a life-threatening scenario. This time when the eaglets fall, their parents are nowhere in sight. *What if they don't show up? What if they don't come through? Has it all been a cruel joke, only to end in this horrible scene?* They can see the headlines now: *Abandoned Eaglets Plunge to Their Death: Eagle Parents Arrested for Murder.* Those kids keep moving their wings, because they don't want to die prematurely.

Then a marvelous thing happens. Nature takes over. Those eaglet wings start moving in slow motion, as the eaglets take off flying for the first time. That's when Father Eagle peeks out from behind the clouds where he has been watching all along, and Mama Eagle smiles from wing to wing as she peers down from her nest.

"Look, Daddy! " the eaglets screech in unison. "We're flying! We're flying! Just like you!"

The time comes in every mother's life when she must begin removing the "feathers" from her child's soft nest. Standing on their own two feet hurts, and the kids may fall numerous times as they move closer to independence. But falling doesn't always mean failing. Unlike the eaglets, sometimes our kids may try to leave the nest too soon. Either way, we try to rescue and forgive as good parents do, giving them more and more freedom until the time comes when they'll leave the nest permanently. Some kids may even get too comfy "resting" and need a few gentle but firm pushes to leave the nest.

Every mom wants their child to grow up just like their Father — reflecting the character of Christ. But every child is unique. Some of them prefer to "test" rather than "rest." Sometimes our kids reject even our most loving efforts to prepare them so they can "fly" through life successfully on their own.

We moms are not on this child-raising journey alone. Mothering is a tough job, but one thing is certain. Our heavenly Father assures us that he is always watching, ready to move at lightning speed and scoop up our children if they will let him. We can commit them to God's care for safekeeping. He is a strong refuge — for us and for them.

And his nest is always best.

DAY-BREAK

Are your children resting, testing, or nesting? How are you preparing them to fly on their own? Challenge your kids to memorize Psalm 91 (you too). Then meditate on the truths in that psalm often as you commit your kids into your heavenly Father's keeping.

DAY-BRIEF

We can give our children roots and wings, but only God can make them fly.

DAY-VOTEDLY YOURS

Heavenly Father, I need you so much! My heart's desire is that my children would grow up to be just like you. Soften their falls with your strong wings of refuge, and teach them how to soar like eagles.

the best gift of all

It is more blessed to give than to receive.
Acts 20:35

Exhausted from stretching the budget, I returned home from the grocery store in tears one day. I had been carefully planning to buy just the right Christmas gift for my husband. However, with a near-zero checkbook balance, I resigned myself to the inevitable and tried to be optimistic. *We can always exchange hugs*, I thought. I knew my daughter's packages would be fewer as well. Would she understand?

What mom doesn't want to give her child the very best of gifts on special occasions, especially Christmas? Yet I had chosen the life of a stay-at-home mom after the birth of our first child, knowing luxuries would be nonexistent.

This was our first full-time ministry position following seminary graduation. We moved to another state and knew no one in this small Arizona military town. Before leaving, we had written down a budget we thought we could survive on as a family of three after Larry graduated. Our figures were modest and we thought they would cover the basic necessities.

We had come in "view of a call," which simply meant the church flew us out for a weekend to consider my husband for a staff position as youth and education director. That Sunday night, we waited in another building while the people voted to determine our worth, um, destiny — as they decided on a salary package to offer us. The amount equaled our simple needs, so Larry accepted the job. Nevertheless, expenses often surpassed income, so we knew we had entered a walk of faith. We tried to watch our budget carefully.

After my experience at the grocery store earlier that day, the subject of finances rose as a hot topic at dinner that evening. After a few minutes of somewhat emotional discussion, my then three-year-old daughter blurted out precociously, "If you want to give money, give it to the missionaries."

We both looked at our daughter and then at each other with a Huh? kind of stare. Her comment made no sense at the moment, but we enjoyed a good laugh, glad that her timely words had ended our debate.

We discovered a greater joy than the exchange of expensive gifts.

But the more I thought about my daughter's wisdom, the more excited I grew. A light bulb turned on in my mind. *Why not?* Carefully, I formed a plan and shared it with Larry that night. Together we made a commitment.

A few days later, we cleaned out our crowded storeroom and discovered several items destined as someone else's treasure. A carport sale combined with an unexpected check in the mail totaled the amount we had pledged earlier for our mission offering.

That Christmas we shared only token gifts with each other. But as we laid our gift to Jesus under the tree — the money for our mission offering — we discovered a greater joy than the exchange of expensive gifts. That night the multicolored lights on the tree seemed to dance with joy, almost as if reflecting the twinkle in my little preschooler's eyes. As we sipped our steaming apple cider and nestled together in our small living room, reading the familiar Christmas story took on a greater meaning.

A little child had led us to the foot of the manger, where heaven touched us. And we saw Jesus — the true Light of the world — with new eyes.

DAY-BREAK

As a mom, how have you handled "lean" times at holidays or special occasions? What are you teaching your children about the blessedness of giving? What can you do this year to renew the real meaning of special days like Christmas?

DAY-BRIEF

It's not what you have but what you give that touches another's life.

DAY-VOTEDLY YOURS

Jesus, you are the reason for any season of my life, and I owe you so much. Help me to remember that you hold the key to making my life meaningful. Teach me as a mom to keep you as the central focus of my life and home every day of the year.

play dates and pray dates

And pray in the Spirit on all occasions with all kinds
of prayers and requests … always keep on praying.
Ephesians 6:18

Years ago a mom could safely shove her kids out the front door for a couple of hours to play with the neighborhood children and not worry about them. The rumbling of the kids' stomachs would usually remind them it was time to stop and come home for dinner. My kids knew the sound of "the bell" (they probably hated it). Wherever they were, down the street, riding bikes, or playing ball, I'd ring a loud metal bell, a relic from some garage sale, and they'd hear it and come running home.

But a child's world today affords less spontaneous play with other kids. To many moms, "play dates" are one of those "inventions of necessity." Perhaps feeling like isolated prisoners of a new culture turned violent and unsafe, moms schedule these events to provide their kids with the social interaction they *both* need — especially if they have young children. The country's increased mobility also influences this new trend, partly because families no longer live close to each other, and miles hinder the opportunity for needed support.

Mothers try diligently to carve out special play times with other kids and their moms, sometimes in their homes or sometimes at a nearby park. The majority of moms schedule play dates for their preschoolers, but many continue the practice as their children start to school, setting "after school dates."

Mothers often connect with other moms in various women's groups, mom's clubs, or special play groups organized through neighborhoods, churches, or even children's clothing stores. In recent years specialized, one-stop children's enrichment centers have sprung up for those wanting more class-oriented play. These kinds of places offer play dates through activities involving gymnastics, art, music, or science.

But a quick look at Mom's fridge calendar shows few blank squares. Church activities, luncheons, doctor's appointments, and work obligations fill most of the spots. It seems like every moment of every day belongs to someone. It will require all her creativity to squeeze in one more activity.

A mom often gives so much that she can soon give out. That's when it's time to reexamine herself, rearrange her life, and schedule time for something else: "pray dates." "What's that?" you ask.

In those early childhood years, planning "pray dates" for yourself will require the same creativity as scheduling play dates for your kids. Even if your calendar does show empty spaces, unless you intentionally plan them as regular events, those moments alone with God won't happen.

I remember trying to find spare moments alone when my kids were preschoolers. I even kept a Bible on the back of the bathroom commode. One day I said to my daughter, "Honey, I'm going in the bathroom to have a few minutes of quiet time with God. (It was the only quiet place I could find at the time.) Will you play in your room for five minutes until Mom comes out?"

But as soon as I opened my Bible, I heard high-pitched musical strains coming from the hallway outside the door: "I'm having my qui-et time. I'm having my qui-et time!" My daughter was having her "quiet time." But unfortunately, I was *not* having mine.

I eventually disciplined myself to get up fifteen to thirty minutes before the kids and "schedule" a walk in the neighborhood while I prayer-walked and talked with God alone. That worked for several years. If you're not an evening *or* morning person and you still have a child at home, you might schedule your divine date during their afternoon nap. (I know, some of you need to catch up on *your* sleep then too!)

Time passes quickly, and kids start school. Your calendar will fill up even more. Whether you're a stay-at-home mom with multiple kids, a mom who works outside her home, or one who conducts a business inside her home, you'll never find extra time just lying around.

One mother I know communes with God as she commutes to work, using praise or Scripture tapes to help her focus. Another turns her lunch hour into a private date with God as she retreats into a garden area or on a company bench. You may even have to enlist friends to help and create a pool of "prayer friends," taking turns keeping kids so each can schedule a solitary, longer prayer date. Timing is between you and God.

The need for formal play dates may cease as kids grow older, but the need for pray dates never ends.

The need for *formal* play dates may cease as kids grow older, but the need for pray dates never ends. I found with every year my desire to spend time alone with God grew stronger. And the times grew longer that I wanted — and needed — to be with him. In fact, my sanity often depended on those dates!

A strange thing happened, though. Throughout the years, my life — and my calendar — left fewer spaces than ever, but God seemed to stretch the rest of the time when I sought him first every day. The length of my pray date always varied, and there were seasons when our "sacred romance" suffered, but God doesn't keep a stopwatch or calendar. It's all about relationship. Your dates may be spontaneous (God loves those too!) or scheduled, but when you seek him first each day, he'll keep your heart soft and your spot warm until you return again. And with him, it's always a safe place to be.

Some days God allowed me to fulfill my obligations more quickly or more efficiently. Other times he showed me ways to eliminate unnecessary tasks, freeing up some spare moments. But he always provided what I needed for that day, because he knew the desire of my heart.

As moms, we're not the only ones who need pray dates. It's an example we can set for our kids as well. We can encourage them to start early (even if it's in the hallway outside the bathroom).

One thing's for sure. Every mom would agree that her pray dates should always include this request: "Lord, help my children never outgrow their need for you!"

DAY-BREAK

How do you create time for your own "pray dates" with God? If this is an area you need to work on, ask God to help you carve out some moments alone with him each day.

DAY-BRIEF

All play and no pray can leave a mom frazzled every day.

DAY-VOTEDLY YOURS

God, you know how much I long for those precious moments with you alone. Show me how to find the time to meet my children's needs as well as my own.

cut the cord!

But the LORD is righteous;
he has cut me free from the cords of the wicked.
Psalm 129:4

For nine months the most amazing nutrition system transmits life to another through a fleshy "IV." Through a thin membrane inside you called the umbilical cord, God provides every physical need your baby has during his or her forming, growing process in the womb.

But when the proper time arrives for your baby to be born, the nine-month source of nutrition ends. The doctor in charge cuts the umbilical cord, and for the first time, your baby must find nourishment on the outside. While still dependent on you for its food, he or she no longer can depend on the cord to supply that.

Can you imagine the disaster of trying to grow that baby without setting it free from its cumbersome cord?

False guilt is like an invisible umbilical cord that's never been cut. When we, by an act of our faith, choose to follow Christ and become his children, we are "reborn" in Christ. God "cuts" the cord of guilt that has long been feeding our sinful nature. Having removed our guilt by his own death and sacrifice, Jesus reminds us as women and mothers that we are free — still dependent on him, but free from the guilt that kept us attached to our old sin nature for so long.

I'm amazed at the number of moms I meet who try to live life with that umbilical cord of guilt still attached. They start off as "newborns," but the demands and pressures of life begin to squeeze off their vibrancy. They listen to negative voices and try to draw nourishment from the wrong sources. Soon wrong beliefs and false guilt begin to consume their thoughts: "I'm not worthy of this!" "I'll never be a good mom!" "Why can't I do better?"

> *False guilt is like an invisible umbilical cord*
> *that's never been cut.*

Our children, eager to please and following our lead, often listen to our comments and develop the same patterns. Watch for clues: your kids may berate themselves or exercise too high expectations of their own capabilities. We as moms can help them overcome their own tendencies to hang onto wrong thinking.

If you find yourself as a mom feeding yourself lies that only lead to disaster, here's a reminder for you: "Cut the cord!" See yourself as Jesus sees you, forgiven, loved, accepted, growing — drawing nutrition from him alone.

Learn the difference between conviction and accusation. The Holy Spirit does not lay false guilt on a child of God, but he does convict us of disobedient actions and wrong thoughts. Ask him to show you the difference between real and false guilt.

Our accuser stands ready night and day to tie us up with cords of his deception. But as our advocate before a holy God, Jesus has the scissors ready. In those times, I wouldn't be surprised to hear him whispering to us in one ear, "Cut the cord!"

It's often a chain reaction. Once you discover that truth, give your children a gift of freedom as well. They must make the decision, but at least you can hand them the (invisible) scissors.

DAY-BREAK

What kind of "lies" have you listened to in the past? In what areas do you need to "cut the cord"? How can you help your children to live in the freedom Christ offers?

DAY-BRIEF

Freedom means living life the way God intended.

DAY-VOTEDLY YOURS

Lord, help me to listen to your words for truth. Thank you for the joy and freedom of being your child. Give me wisdom so I can help my children make good choices that will ensure their freedom and success.

day 13

sleepless in the battle

When you lie down, your sleep will be sweet.
Proverbs 3:24

We had nearly two thousand miles to travel — from Tucson to Atlanta. We considered flying, but the budget couldn't stand it. So, with two preschoolers in tow, we headed across country for our two-day journey. We might not have braved such a trip had we known what that experience would entail.

About thirty miles out of town, our two-and-a-half-month-old daughter Jen let out a series of wails that would have grounded the most experienced traveler. I tried singing, rocking, patting, praying — nothing helped. A bottle didn't satisfy either. Each time I'd stick a pacifier in her mouth, it would fly out at record speed. Every fifty miles we'd stop just to regain our sanity, each taking a turn at walking this colicky infant. Her cries would subside for a few moments, and then grow into full-blown screeches again the moment we pulled back onto the highway.

The entire time I had been pregnant in our small town, I had gone to a young obstetrician. I felt he was not as "old-fashioned" as his father, a grandfatherly figure with whom he shared his practice. And I was still fairly new to the town, so I had my own ideas about childbirth. On a few visits I ended up seeing the older doctor in spite of my preferences. One day I asked if the younger doctor would please deliver my daughter when the due date arrived.

But it didn't happen that way. At four o'clock one morning my husband Larry was walking beside my cart through the small hospital corridor listening to me holler between panting, "Somebody call the doctor. I'm gonna have this baby!" With my first child, the doctor had given me a general anesthetic, and I missed everything. This time, I had prepared for natural childbirth.

The only doctor in town was, you guessed it, Grandfather Doc. But at that moment I couldn't have cared less. He arrived just in the nick of time; I pushed twice, and Jen was born. On one follow-up visit, my grandfatherly doctor had suggested a little whiskey and honey if our baby ever had stomach ailments like colic. Unfortunately, infant Mylicon® gas drops hadn't hit the market yet. Being an upright preacher's wife, I humorously commented that our deacons might think the use of whiskey was good reason for dismissal.

> *There are times in a mom's life when nerves give out and God's sense of humor steps in.*

But at that moment I was desperate. I would have gladly given my baby a drop of the doctor's recipe for just a little relief.

Jen managed to sleep for a few minutes at a time — enough to give us a little respite for our nerves. But by the time we arrived at my parents' home two days later, I eagerly handed her to Mother's

waiting arms. Our baby seemed to brighten at the change of sur-
roundings, and we had no more trouble the rest of the visit.

The days passed quickly — too quickly. I dreaded the trip back
home across the desert.

Maybe she'll sleep soundly this time. Lord, let her sleep, puhleaze!
I silently prayed. Others told me that car motion soothed usually
crying babies. In fact, to get Val, our older daughter, to sleep when
she was only a toddler, I remember on one vacation driving up and
down the hills of Oklahoma at midnight. And it worked. She'd
settle down and conk out as soon as we turned back the bed covers
at our motel.

Unfortunately, that didn't work for Jen. It seemed before we'd
even driven out of my parents' driveway, her whimpers started.
"Here we go again," I complained.

Late that day we arrived at my sister's house, tired and in need
of comfort. Jen had cried the entire day. We immediately told Pat
our scenario. My brother-in-law, whose dry wit had entertained us
on many occasions, was listening from the other room. He walked
calmly to the phone and picked it up.

"I have a friend who has just the thing," he said to us
reassuringly.

Before we could protest, Clovis called a man in his bass club,
and we overheard his conversation: "Bill, my brother-in-law is a
Baptist preacher and he needs a little something to calm his nerves.
You got any whiskey at your house?"

After a few howls of needed laughter, we listened as Clovis

rescued our reputation and explained the real situation. His friend had no whiskey, but he did keep a little brandy for such emergencies. Within minutes, we gratefully mixed up a drop of brandy and honey and spooned it into our baby's mouth. We left the next morning. For the rest of the trip we heard nary a sound from our infant's mouth. She was too busy sleeping.

There are times in a mom's life when nerves give out and God's sense of humor steps in. This was one of those times. Our emotional load was lightened, our reputation was intact, and God helped us sleep peacefully that night ourselves (without the brandy, of course — though the thought did cross my mind a time or two ...).

As to my grandfatherly doctor? I'm pretty sure I swallowed my pride and gave him a huge hug the next time I saw him.

DAY-BREAK

When have your nerves been tested as a mom? How has humor helped to diffuse uptight situations? How has God ministered to you on sleepless nights?

DAY-BRIEF

When all else fails, laugh. It may not change the situation, but it will help you.

DAY-VOTEDLY YOURS

Father, thank you for the gift of laughter. Help me to trust you patiently with every solution, especially when I'm stretched thin with impossible situations.

day 14
truth or consequences

I have no greater joy than to hear
that my children are walking in the truth.
3 John 4

In one particular episode of *Seventh Heaven*, a television series about the ups and downs of a preacher's family, Ruthie and her boyfriend got tattoos. Ruthie hated hers and immediately regretted her weak moment as a stupid mistake. She unwittingly told some of her friends, who also blabbed to her sister Lucy.

As it turned out, all the kids of the Camden family had visited a tattoo parlor at one time or another in their lives, and all had succeeded in hiding their needled designs from their parents. The high cost made tattoo removals prohibitive, so they had to live with them, along with the fear that their parents couldn't handle the truth if they found out. After all, their father had strongly told them "no way" when they asked about tattoos in the past. So they continued to live with guilt, hiding the truth from them.

But Ruthie's mom and dad figured out the reason for Ruthie's secretive behavior — just as they did for all their kids in the past. They just never told the kids they knew. Mom and Dad finally decided to ease up on the charade, but not before putting pressure on the two still close by — Ruthie at home, and Lucy living in the house behind them.

When the parents confessed, the kids — Lucy particularly — couldn't believe that their parents had put them through the torture of guilt, when the parents knew all along what they had done.

At the end of the show, Mom and Dad showed only the television viewers (not the kids) why they never made a big deal about their kids' tattoos — why they didn't force the truth all those years. They turned their backs to the audience and showed their waistlines, revealing their own secret: they both had tattoos as well.[6]

Kids go to great lengths to hide things from their parents. All of us have done the same thing. It may not have been tattoos, but we all succeeded in keeping secrets from our parents — or so we thought.

If we let "tattoos" represent a greater picture, we might call those secret marks our sinful behavior. And kids and moms are not the only ones who try hiding them from each other. We've played that game with God. In a weak moment we made a poor choice; we disobeyed God and paid a ridiculous price for our "tattoos." As it turns out, our stupid mistakes weren't worth the effort — or price. But trying to hide those marks, those memories of sin so engraved in our hearts and minds forever, is even more ridiculous.

*A mother's heart, like the heart of God,
desires nothing more than for her children to live in
freedom and joy, discerning truth, and choosing right.*

Our parents may or may not have known about our secret sins, but God does. He doesn't miss a thing. The difference is, he doesn't want us to go on suffering with guilt and shame. In reality, you don't want your children to, either — no matter how rebellious they may appear at the time. Why? Because a mother's heart, like the heart of God, desires nothing more than for her children to live in freedom and joy, discerning truth, and choosing right.

And whether your kids choose the same "tattoos" as you did or not, you can't pay a price to remove those sin marks permanently. You can't make yours — or theirs — disappear.

But God already made that possible. When you agreed with him about what you had done, he used the ultimate removal tool — his own Son's life — to erase any trace of sin burned into your life. Then he exchanged your sin for his perfection. And if you ask him, he will show you the marks. He knew about your sin all along.

If you've accepted his gift — the price of his own life — your "tattoo" is now engraved on the palms of his hands forever.

DAY-BREAK

Have you ever tried to hide from God? What was the result? How do you encourage your children to be truthful?

DAY-BRIEF

A scar can hide something that was painful — or reveal something that has been healed.

DAY-VOTEDLY YOURS

Jesus, thank you for your healing grace in the lives of my children and me. Keep the horizontal and vertical communication lines open for all of us — that we might live honestly and openly before each other.

their day will come

You do not understand what I am doing,
but later you will understand.
John 13:7

One year when my daughter was in elementary school, I observed a play for one of the first grade reading groups in which my daughter was one of the participants. The voices had been pre-taped, so the children pantomimed the entire story.

The play told of a king who was seeking to find a unicorn worthy to be a good helper for his kingdom. Having secretly set up several "tests" for the three competing unicorns, the king sent them on their way to determine a winner. The first test was a foot race.

As the race progressed, the unicorns encountered several obstacles — a kitten trapped in a tree, an old fisherman whose net was caught in the stream, and a boy hopelessly stuck in the mud. The first two unicorns paused, but were too busy to stop and help. They wanted only to finish the race first to become the king's helper.

However, the third unicorn stopped each time to help relieve the distress of those who had met with difficulties, even though he knew it might mean losing the race.

At the end of the race, all of the three unicorns waited eagerly for the king's decision.

"The true winner is … the *third* unicorn!" said the king. "She is the only one who took time to help."

Hmm. This sounds like the story of the Good Samaritan, I thought to myself. *What a great lesson for children at this age to learn!*

When the skit was finished, the young reading teacher turned to her first grade audience and said, "Now boys and girls, what lesson can we learn from this story?"

Parents held their breath and waited expectantly, confident that their child would volunteer and nail the obvious, most important lesson gleaned from the play.

From the back one eager youngster shot up his hand. "I know! I know!" he yelled out with pride. "Don't play in the mud!"

As a mom, you may feel like that's the story of your lives. All the lessons you teach your kids seem to go in one ear and exit with a totally different meaning. *Maybe a few years will make a difference,* you think. But childhood passes. And not only do your teenagers not get it; they don't even *hear* you.

Jesus' disciples sometimes acted the same way. Taught by a perfect Master, the Son of God, they still missed the point. They didn't understand. Jesus constantly used stories, or parables, to illustrate his important truths. But most of the time when Jesus ended a parable, his disciples stood there, scratching their heads with a "Huh?" or discussing the possible meaning among themselves. They just didn't "get" it.

One day all the "stories" you told them,
all the lessons you taught, all the truths you wanted
to burn in their memory will make sense.

At one point Jesus even asked them, "Don't you understand this parable? How then will you understand any parable?" (Mark 4:13). Sounds like a true parent's synopsis.

But Jesus never gave up teaching, training, or loving them. When they didn't understand why he would wash their feet, Jesus simply replied knowingly, "Later you will understand."

But it took awhile. Jesus' miracles amazed them, but his stories confused them. His talk of persecution, of his own death, of a Comforter he would send to them, and of a place he would prepare for them — Jesus knew they could not fully grasp these things until a later time (John 14:16). He knew that when all was said and done and in God's special timing, a light bulb would turn on. The Holy Spirit would come in his place and fill their hearts and minds, reminding them of his powerful words.

We too as moms can only trust that in God's special timing, his Spirit will illumine the hearts and minds of our own children. I'll never forget the day our oldest daughter called us from college. In one of her classes she was involved in a heated discussion about some important issues. Val said to us, "You know, it's pretty scary. I found myself saying things *you* would say!"

One day all the "stories" you told them, all the lessons you taught, all the truths you wanted to burn into their memory will make sense. You may have to wait awhile. There are some things kids won't fully understand until they're parenting their own children. And then the light dawns: "Oh, yeah! That's what Mom was talking about!"

It may take a long time. But keep holding on to the truth Jesus offered his own disciples. Understanding will come. And when it does, it will be worth the wait.

DAY-BREAK

What lessons and truths do you especially want your kids to understand? This week, take time to pray for your children. And each time you "catch" them applying a truth you've taught them, brag on them — and give God thanks!

DAY-BRIEF

When faith opens the door, hope walks in.

DAY-VOTEDLY YOURS

Lord, thank you that when I wait, I am not alone. You are always there, encouraging me as a mom to keep patiently teaching and guiding my children. Keep them near to your heart and illumine their minds so they can always apply your truth in every situation.

day 16
spiritual myopia

*And Elisha prayed, "Open his eyes, LORD, so that he may see." Then
the LORD opened the servant's eyes, and he looked and saw the hills
full of horses and chariots of fire all around Elisha.*
2 Kings 6:17

"Lift me up, Daddy! I can't see!"

The parade was coming closer, and I didn't want to miss the
multicolored floats, the spontaneous clowns, or the amazing per-
formers as they edged our way. I was only a small child, and too
short to see through the sea of legs in front of me. So with huge,
strong arms, my daddy, who stood six feet four inches, gently lifted
me up so I could see the parade.

We moms have trouble seeing God's beautiful "parades" in life
too. But it's not because we're too short. It's because we're too shortsighted. Our physical eyes are open, but our spiritual eyes remain
closed. Hidden fears block our view, and faith can't seem to find
an opening.

That's what happened to Elisha's servant. The king of Aram's
(Syria) plans to attack Israel repeatedly went awry, and he sus-
pected an informant within his own ranks. When he discovered
the traitor was none other than Elisha, a prophet of God, the king
reacted. Elisha had been intercepting messages from God related

to the Syrians' attacks and had passed on the information to the king of Israel.

Enraged, the Syrian king sent an army of soldiers by night to surround the city where Elisha lived. When Elisha's servant rose up early and saw the huge army, he panicked with fear.

But Elisha, with a calm and trusting assurance in his God, prayed that God would open his servant's eyes so he could see. Immediately, the scales of disbelief fell from his eyes, and he was able to see a host of heavenly angels surrounded by horses and chariots of fire. The battle was supernatural, and God would fight it for them (2 Kings 6:8 – 17).

Many of us, like the servant, suffer from spiritual myopia, an eye condition that causes improper focus and poor vision. We can see our kids' weaknesses, our family's problems, and our own inabilities. But they seem to be standing in front of us like a sea of giant legs, or a giant army of enemies, blocking a clear view.

> *Only God can heal our spiritual myopia and open our eyes of faith to see him working on our behalf.*

Because of our improper focus on them, our vision is limited. We're focusing on the problems, not on the provision. The servant saw a horde of Syrians, but Elisha saw a host of angels.

If we as moms focus only on our problems and difficulties, we will miss not only God's provision; we will miss his parade. Fear and worry stifle beauty and block the path of faith. Who wants to go through life shortsighted, missing God's everyday celebrations — multicolored memories, spontaneous laughter, and amazing moments God has designed for us — and our families?

Only God can heal our spiritual myopia and open our eyes of faith to see him working on our behalf. Only God can lift us up with strong, steady arms so we can see his purpose clearly. Only God can help us enjoy the parade he created for us.

But he'll do it only if we ask.

DAY-BREAK

What causes you to be shortsighted at times and focus on your own problems rather than on God's provision? Describe some of the "parades" God has created for you and allowed you and your family to enjoy.

DAY-BRIEF

Trying to see without faith is like walking in the dark.

DAY-VOTEDLY YOURS

God, forgive me for the times I've let doubt, fear, or difficulties block my vision. You are more than able to fight my battles for me. Open my eyes that I might truly see my family and my future with eyes of faith.

day 17
taming the untamable

Consider what a great forest is set on fire by a small spark.
The tongue also is a fire … It corrupts the whole person,
sets the whole course of one's life on fire.
James 3:5 – 6

I left the kitchen for only a moment. Two burners kept overheating, which made cooking more difficult. I thought I had removed the skillet of grease from the hot burner when I left the room.

A few minutes later my daughter careened through the hallway yelling, "Mom, come quick! There's a fire in the kitchen!"

Thinking she meant a small oven fire from drippings (I also had a casserole baking in the oven), I walked calmly back into the kitchen. But I let out a gasp when I saw flames leaping up almost to the ceiling, directly above the skillet that I had accidentally left on the burner.

We tried to cover the skillet with the lid, but it was warped and wouldn't cover the flames. Somehow we managed to remove the skillet from the stove and apply a nearby fire extinguisher. That put the fire out immediately, but billows of smoke filled our entire home.

We surveyed the damage. The fire scorched some of the cabinets, floor, and oven, but we were so grateful to escape harm and more serious problems. Restoring our kitchen would require an intense cleanup. I had just finished wallpapering one wall, and that entire space was covered with soot, along with the ceiling. We spent the remainder of the evening scrubbing away the smoke residue and the next day repainting the ceiling. Repapering followed later.

God's Word says the tongue is like that flame started by an innocent, yet careless mistake. If we can't "put a lid" on our tongues and we continue to spew out anger, those words can never be retrieved. A fire erupts. And before we know it, out-of-control flames have caused internal damage. No mom knowingly wants to destroy those she loves with an untamable tongue.

> *As mothers, we can contribute to the loving and safe atmosphere in our homes through the power of our positive words.*

When we as moms and women use wagging tongues to repeat morsels of gossip, half-truths, or words that tear down our kids, our husbands, or others, lives can be destroyed in one thoughtless moment. Even constant complaints can be the sparks that set our home on "fire."

As mothers, we can contribute to the loving and safe atmosphere in our homes through the power of our positive words. Our kids need to hear kindness from our tongues, thoughtful and encouraging affirmations that build up, not tear down. The Bible is full of such words.

Kyle Dodd, a speaker at the February 2009 Family Life Weekend to Remember Conference in Dallas, offered a good solution to help keep our tongues in check. He described a nocturnal crane, unique to the Taurus Mountains in Turkey, whose long tongue made a loud, cackling or clacking noise against its beak as it flew. Predators, such as the eagle, would hear that clacking in the dark night and know exactly where to swoop down and capture that crane for its supper. The crane's tongue led to its own self-destruction!

But apparently the crane figured out a way to "tame," or silence, its unruly tongue. It would pick up a stone and lodge it strategically under its tongue. Voila! The cackling and clacking stopped — and the crane's predators could no longer locate it in the dark.[7]

The tongue is such a small member of our body, but what a powerful force! What can we as moms do to tame it? Perhaps we could all learn from the Turkish crane. The next time you start to open your mouth and let the "clacking" begin, grab a "rock" from God's Word and hide it under your tongue (and in your heart).

The sweetness and power of his truths will extinguish any flames before they begin — and help ward off any temptations waiting to devour you and your family.

DAY-BREAK

Have you ever uttered unkind words to your children or gossiped about someone? How did it make you feel afterward? How did it affect others? Find two other Bible verses that you can use as "rocks" to put under your tongue this week. Speak positive words of affirmations to your children, husband, and others that you meet today.

DAY-BRIEF

A "cackle" a day may keep your family away.

DAY-VOTEDLY YOURS

Father, guard my tongue and keep my words sweet. Thank you for the power of your Word and for the precious privilege of leading my children closer to you.

day 18
this too shall pass

There is a time for everything,
and a season for every activity under the heavens.
Ecclesiastes 3:1

Kerry snuggled in her backyard swing, swaying gently back and forth. Robins and blue jays perched on the empty branches of her tall oak trees and chirped noisily, as if to say, "Hurry up, spring. We're ready!"

Kerry was ready too. Mothering at all hours of the night had left her exhausted. *Do babies ever sleep through the night?* A misty fog hung, suspended in the sky, as a winter chill crept through her body. She pulled her warm blanket closer. *That's me — in a fog, Lord. Springtime is coming. But will I ever experience it?*

In another state, miles away, Cathy pulled back the curtains of her bedroom window. A flurry of leaves fell from the trees like brown and gold snowflakes. Trees, once green, now stood half naked, devoid of their once-held grandeur. The seasons were changing, just like her life. She had known middle age would not be easy — that her teenage children's years would be challenging — but not like this season. The last few weeks had been a nightmare as her kids made one bad decision after another.

Her hormones — and theirs — seemed to clash every month like planes on a crash course.

And why did God choose to take her beloved husband home just when she needed him the most? It had only been a few months, but to her, time had stood still forever. She crawled back in bed and pulled the covers over her head. *After fall, comes winter. What else is around the corner, Lord? When will it end? Will I ever make it through?*

Two moms, different, yet alike. Both faced difficult seasons; yet each one struggled with circumstances unique to her stage in life. You've been there, haven't you? The seasons of motherhood change, but they never end. Problems come and go, like the children in our home. How do we cope with each one? I often wondered the same thing as a mother. One year I found the encouragement I needed as I poured out my heart to God onto the pages of my journal:

> *What season is it now, Lord? Winter? Fall? Spring?*
> *A time to hibernate and rest? A time for me to sing?*
> *How do I fit into your scheme? When will this season pass?*
> *How long before you answer? How long will these times last?*
> *The seeds have long been planted; my roots are growing deep.*
> *But the leaves are starting to wither. How long before I reap?*
> *The weeds have choked their years from me; I need the spring-*
>   *time rain.*
> *I long to see new flowers bloom, where once grew only pain.*
> *When questions go unanswered; when life's a mystery,*

*I know one thing will never change, and that's your love for
 me.
I cannot make a garden grow by struggling on my own;
But I can lift my petals high, and let you bring the growth.*

Every mother will experience a time or times when a certain
season seems to last forever. But there is a reason for every season — and a purpose for every event and circumstance that God
allows to enter our lives.

Other moms may not experience your same situation, but they
can identify with the struggle. One mother fairly flies through
childhood with easy babies, then almost crashes and burns when
her kids enter adolescence. One woman raises easy-going teens,
but her grown-up kids turn into impossible prodigals. Birth, death,
planting, reaping; weeping, laughing, mourning, dancing; keeping,
discarding, loving, hating — Ecclesiastes says there's a time for all
these things and more.

> *But there is a reason for every season —
> and a purpose for every event and circumstance
> that God allows to enter our lives.*

But I love verse 11 of Ecclesiastes 3: "He has made everything
beautiful in its time." Your winters will pass away as daffodils
poke their heads up through hard, dry soil. The leaves will cease
to fall, and new buds will replace the barren limbs once again. You
will laugh again. And you *will* cry again. But through it all — and

sometimes after it all — you will look back and see the faithful Creator's hand at work.

Remember, creating beauty out of ashes is God's specialty. It's all a matter of his timing.

DAY-BREAK

What season are you in right now? What is your favorite time of year? When has God brought beauty out of ashes for you? Take time today to journal about the season of life you are in and ask God to help you see the blessings in it.

DAY-BRIEF

Only one "season" lasts forever: eternity.

DAY-VOTEDLY YOURS

Lord, help me remember that you are in charge of the seasons of my life. I want to celebrate the good ones and learn from the difficult ones. Thank you that the season for loving my children never ends. You taught me that, Lord, by your own example.

day 19
small offerings,
big rewards

*Here is a boy with five small barley loaves and two small fish,
but how far will they go among so many?*
John 6:9

After living in Arizona for fifteen years, we moved back to our
native state of Texas. Our girls had gone to Christian school much
of that time, but reentered public school when we returned. One
was in junior high, the other in high school. To save money, I often
packed homemade lunches and sent them with the girls to school.
I often tucked a handwritten note or Bible verse into their bags to
encourage them.

I continued the practice after we moved to the Dallas metro-
plex, but one day my girls confessed their school friends' comments
when they first saw the homey lunches and notes: "Oh, how *cute*!"
I guess I was a little naïve not to realize I might be embarrass-
ing them with my offerings, but the girls never seemed to mind.
(Until later as adults. They admitted humorously that it wasn't the
notes or taking a lunch or even their friends' remarks that bothered
them. It was the fact that I only put one thin piece of lunchmeat
on their bread!)

Another mom packed a lunch one day for her son — more than one thin sandwich, but still a small offering. The bag contained five small barley loaves and two fish. Sounds about right for a growing boy's appetite. But it's not what the boy's peers thought about his lunch that mattered that day; it's what the Teacher thought. Jesus' disciples crossed it off simply as a small boy's lunch. But when the boy surrendered all of his meal willingly to Jesus, something miraculous happened. Jesus took the contents of that lunch bag and fed five thousand men, plus women and children. Can you imagine the size of that boy's eyes as he watched his lunch keep growing and growing and growing?

Every word you speak, every lunch you pack,
every lesson you teach, and every hug you give
are like a small fish or barley loaf
that God can and will multiply.

We moms may cross off the little things we do for our kids as mundane tasks that don't really count for much. Fixing meals, changing diapers, applying Band-aid kisses, helping them with homework. We tuck into their day small words of encouragement each time they leave home: "Have a good day!" "I'm praying for you!" "I love you!" "Don't forget your coat!" But nothing is too small in God's eyes.

I bet that mom never realized that day when she packed her son's lunch that she — and her son — would feed a multitude. She only planned to feed her son. But Jesus turned her simple task into an event that has literally touched millions and millions of people through the years as they read about that miracle in the Bible.

Who packed Billy Graham's lunch each day when he was a boy? And what about the mom who fed Mordecai Ham, the evangelist who introduced Billy to Jesus? How many millions of people have come to know Jesus because of the influence of two moms who raised these two young men?

Your child may not grow up to be as prominent as a CEO, a United States president, or an evangelist like Billy Graham, but you as a mom are part of a bigger picture in God's plan. Every word you speak, every lunch you pack, every lesson you teach, and every hug you give are like a small fish or barley loaf that God can and will multiply.

Be faithful. Nothing you do is ordinary or just "cute." You *are* making a difference in your child's life. And if what you provide for your kids is given with love, you'll be amazed at what God will do with your influence — no matter how thin a slice of life you have to offer.

DAY-BREAK

Think about the things you do for your children. How many do you consider mundane? Ask God to transform everything you do for them as an offering of thanksgiving. And today, just for fun, tuck a note of encouragement somewhere into their day.

DAY-BRIEF

Giving your all — is never small.

DAY-VOTEDLY YOURS

Jesus, help me to view the simple tasks of motherhood with new eyes. Take my small offerings, Lord, and multiply them to grow godly children who love you passionately.

it takes so little

*If you, then, though you are evil, know how to give good gifts
to your children, how much more will your Father in heaven
give good gifts to those who ask him!*
Matthew 7:11

"Mom, how come *we* don't get to dress up and go to dinner at a special restaurant?"

My daughter Val usually tried to make holidays special for the entire family — including Valentine's Day. But her husband, Shawn, also enjoyed treating her to a Valentine meal at a nice restaurant, just for the two of them. When Val heard her son's comment on Valentine's Day, she varied from her usual planned gifts.

This particular Valentine's Day, Val and Shawn had already gone out for a nice Valentine lunch. But this year, to save money and avoid the crowds, Val decided to prepare a special steak dinner for the two of them later that evening at home. They planned to feed the kids early and then enjoy their meal after the kids were asleep.

Their son commented on their lunch date out earlier and then observed them making the special preparations ahead of time that evening: candles on the table, fancy tablecloth, and china. That's when he asked the question about a kids' dinner out.

Val and Shawn looked at each other, and like spontaneous combustion, their eyes twinkled as their creative minds started churning. They nodded in agreement to each other and said, "You know what? How about tomorrow night the two of *you* dress up and you can go to a fancy restaurant for dinner too!"

"We'll take you to Stinky Pants Italian Restaurant," chimed in Shawn. (You'd have to know him and the kids to realize how much those children love his crazy, offbeat humor!)

Val says if money is an issue, this plan works well, because you can always find half-price Valentine chocolate, trinkets, and decorations at most local discount or drug stores the day after Valentine's. That's exactly what she did.

So the kids couldn't wait until the following evening. Shawn dressed up in his chef outfit, and together they worked on the kids' favorite meal: spaghetti and meatballs. Val baked brownies and cut them out in heart shapes, ready to serve with a scoop of ice cream for desert. While dinner simmered, she even grabbed her camera and snapped a picture of Shawn in his chef hat. She then escaped to her office and created a quick menu for the table. On the front was a picture of Chef Stinky Pants (Shawn) and the restaurant's name: "Stinky Pants Italian Restaurant," along with the menu outline.

The kids dressed up in their Sunday best clothes, and with great fanfare their parents served them their own special Valentine meal by candlelight. It was a memory they won't soon forget.

Remember our Father loves to give good gifts too.

Creating fun memories for children and making kids feel special don't always require a chunk out of the budget — or even excessive planning. Spontaneity may not come easy for you. But with a little creativity, you can come up with your own ideas unique to your and your kids' own personalities.

It really takes so little to please kids, especially if you model that yourself. The next time your children ask for something special, think twice before saying no — especially if it's not really a selfish request and won't require an expensive or impossible solution. Remember, our Father loves to give good gifts too.

Florence Littauer once wrote a book called *It Takes So Little to Be above Average.* A child may need to plant the seed of creativity in some of us, but when we go the extra mile and say to our kids, "You really are special!" we're not the only ones who will feel "above average."

Our kids will too.

DAY-BREAK

How do you make your kids feel special? What can you do to turn holidays into "above average" celebrations?

DAY-BREAK

With children, always wear "kid" gloves.

DAY-VOTEDLY YOURS

Lord, thank you for every good gift you give to my family and me. Help me as a mom to find ways to say yes to my children and to treat them as special gifts themselves.

day 21
sex after kids?

I have taken off my robe —
must I put it on again? . . .
Many waters cannot quench love;
rivers cannot sweep it away.

Song of Songs 5:3; 8:7

"Hi, I'm Jill Savage. My husband, Mark, and I have been married nineteen years, nine of them happily."

That's what Jill, a mom, speaker, and founder of *Hearts at Home* ministry, wrote in the opening statement of her book *Is There Really Sex after Kids?* Jill says her marriage "was a mess during the first ten years . . . a mess we both created by our selfishness, anger, pride, and criticism."

They sought counseling after their seventh anniversary, and part of their help included sexual counseling. Jill says, "At that time, I couldn't have cared less about sex. I was knee deep in diapers and dishes. Making meat loaf was a higher priority than making love."[8]

Jill's work with women revealed she was not the only mom who has struggled with sexual intimacy in marriage. In fact, it's probably safe to say that all women deal with it at some time or another — even the wife in Song of Songs.

What happened between the "covers" of her statement: "I have taken off my robe — must I put it on again?" and her confession a few chapters later: "Many waters cannot quench love"? She has already retired for the night when her husband comes "knocking" at her door with that gleam in his eye. His hand is on the door, and he is trying to open it. For a moment she rethinks her tiredness. But by the time she moves to the door, he is gone. The opportunity has passed (Song of Songs 5:4 – 6).

As a mom and wife, you might have experienced at least part of that scenario. But you were too exhausted to "rethink" anything. Unfortunately, by the time your husband opened the door you were asleep. For some of you, the door of sexual intimacy not only closed; it has stayed locked for years.

Is there really sex after kids, as Jill wrote about? How can you, as a mom, raise lovemaking to a higher priority than making meat loaf (or at least equal it)? How can you squeeze sex between the sheets of an already overloaded bed full of diapers, dolls, and dirty laundry?

You can read books like Kevin Leman's *Sex Begins in the Kitchen*, Gary Chapman's *The Five Love Languages*, and of course, Jill's book. There are tons of resources available. Read the Song of Songs thoroughly to see the vitality of a strong, intimate relationship between husband and wife. This devotion you're reading only cracks the door — to discussion.

But only when you transfer knowledge to experience will things improve. Above all, don't let problems simmer. It's true, seasons will pass, and your children will one day be grown, but a couple who has never stoked the fire during the earlier years may find the flame has gone out when their nest has emptied.

Sexual intimacy begins with a spiritual and emotional oneness.

Every mom can work on her schedule, simplifying what she can to make time for the love of her life. Locks on the bedroom door (to keep the kids out, not your husband), creating "down" time for yourself to recharge your batteries, and daily husband-wife check-ins to communicate on a deeper level will help. Learning each other's love language, sharing household tasks together, praying through the problems, and planning ahead for special, creative times can free up time and energy to invest into each other.

If you're constantly drained at night as a mom, vary the times you make love. Larry and I tucked our small kids into bed at 7:30 most nights without apology. If they objected, we replied, "We need your sleep more than you do." We've been fortunate through the years to live close to Larry's workplace, so he could come home for lunch most days. Once kids are in school, some distractions are gone, and energy is often at a higher peak during the day. Don't be afraid to initiate. The woman in Song of Songs realized how much she loved her man, so she rose and pursued him!

If you both work full-time, your challenges are even greater as a mom. But the key is working on your relationship together.

Remember that having sex is not necessarily the same as sharing sexual intimacy. If deeper, emotional issues lie beneath the surface, talk about them honestly to each other. Women who experienced sexual abuse or were taught early on that sex was something dirty, unpleasant, or simply a "duty" may need professional help seeing God's beautiful plan and purpose for the sexual relationship in marriage. Men steeped in pornography can make their wives feel more like sex objects than loving, intimate partners. Fear of pregnancy or pain or emotional overload can easily shut the door as well. But an openness in sharing and truly working together will help deepen your relationship.

Sexual intimacy begins with a spiritual and emotional oneness. Talk about this part of your relationship together. Don't spend your married life "dropping clues" or trying to guess what the other one wants or likes. Commit your relationship to God.

Accept your differences as husband and wife. Jill Savage says, "Men think about sex once every seventeen seconds." But according to her friend Jane, "Women think about sex once every seventeen days — and that's on a good month."[9] While God didn't wire men and women the same way, he did create them both in his image with freedom to enjoy an intimate relationship as husband and wife.

It will take both of you with God's help to make it through the rough waters, especially during the childbearing years. But you can. And as you do, the next time you hear that knock on the door, you may find yourself agreeing with the woman in Song of Songs: "Neither rain nor sleet, nor snow nor dark of night can wash away our love" (Song of Songs 8:7, author's — and postal service's — paraphrase).

And hopefully this time, there'll be a gleam in both of your eyes as you throw open the door and exclaim with genuine enthusiasm, "Come in!"

DAY-BREAK

What hinders your sexual intimacy the most as a mom? How

do you keep this area of your life vital and growing? What will you do this week to make sex pleasurable for both you and your husband?

DAY-BRIEF

Intimacy means seeing into me.

DAY-VOTEDLY YOURS

Lord, help me to remember that my husband's needs are as important as my own. Keep our love as fresh and as new as the first day we married, but help us to deepen it daily as we grow more intimately in love with each other.

day 22
one day at a time

Therefore do not worry about tomorrow, for tomorrow will worry about itself. Each day has enough trouble of its own.
Matthew 6:34

"Yes, uh-huh, Oh, really? Good." The one-sided conversation I was having with my young daughter soon ended in silence as she slipped away quietly to her room.

Suddenly I realized that we had been in two different places. My eyes were looking at my daughter, but my mind was focusing on yesterday, tomorrow, or my unfinished work for the day. Perhaps she sensed my half-hearted efforts at conversation and left frustrated.

I wish I could say that was an isolated incident, but there were multiple times when my mind has wandered in the middle of others' conversations, running toward yesterday's events or to plans for tomorrow. Perhaps all of us as moms find ourselves in situations where we would rather not be, and we catch our thoughts, wishing we could escape or hoping for the time to pass quickly so we can get on with "more important" things. I've heard other moms say, "If I could just ..." or "When I get past this problem, or this week, or this day ..."

The secret of contentment is fairly simple. It's realizing that God has already provided everything we need for our present happiness. The apostle Paul encourages us not to "worry about anything" and to "pray about everything" (Philippians 4:6 LB).

It's easy for moms to wish away their lives — or their kids' years, especially when they're struggling with the "terrible twos" or rebellious teens. "Enjoy them now!" we hear our own moms exhorting us. "They'll be gone before you know it." And we nod politely, secretly wondering if we'll ever see a break on the horizon. Some mothers live in the past, holding onto impossible realities, while others look to the future for that better day when life might be easier or circumstances might change.

But God says all we're promised is right now — today — the present. Learning to live one day at a time can affect our whole attitude if we only let that truth sink in.

Live every day as if it were the first day of your life, and as if it were your last.

Looking back now, I realize our moms were right. The years do pass too quickly. I did my share of wishing away seasons of pain and inconvenience. But I also learned the joy of relationship. After scores of frustrated attempts, I eventually got the hang of listening better (though I'm always working on it). And I've long since dropped the habit of trying to live in the past. I can't change yesterday, but I can learn from it. And why worry about tomorrow? There's enough to deal with today. That doesn't mean I can't *plan* for the future, but I don't have to be consumed or bothered with the "what ifs."

The psalmist reiterated the importance of contentment: "This is the day the LORD has made; let us rejoice and be glad in it" (Psalm 118:24 NIV). One thing about growing older is that you do learn to appreciate the present. But whether you're a young, a middle-aged, or an older mom, it's not too late. Live every day as if it were the first day of your life, and as if it were your last. When your children talk, listen — really listen. When you're with your family or with others, really be there — not somewhere else. Consciously focus on their needs and concerns as well as the enjoyment of the moment. It will pass too quickly — and so will they.

Today may be all you have, so live it with purpose and meaning and with the smile of God upon it. If you do, contentment will fill your heart each day. And others may start asking about your secret — even your kids.

DAY-BREAK

When are you most often tempted to wish away the years? What keeps you most distracted from giving your full attention to your kids, to your husband, or to others? Today, list three reasons for being content in this season of your life.

DAY-BRIEF

Today is a precious treasure. Don't bury it and forget where you put it.

DAY-VOTEDLY YOURS

God, each time I'm tempted to live in the past or future, remind me of your grace and mercy for today. Teach me to live one day at a time so I can model true contentment to my own children.

always in school

Fix these words of mine in your hearts and minds ...
Teach them to your children, talking about them
when you sit at home and when you walk along the road,
when you lie down and when you get up.
Deuteronomy 11:18 – 19

I've always heard "a picture is worth a thousand words," but after one particular experience I would add that a living illustration is worth just as much. One evening my young girls and I were shopping at a large department store. As we entered through the automatic doors, an attendant leaned over to check a package of mine (I was planning to match some fabric).

Out of the corner of my eye I spotted a large, dignified-looking man motion to the tall stocky attendant. At the same time I noticed a rather short young man in his early twenties, dressed in jeans and T-shirt, walking briskly out the exit door. Before I knew what was happening, the store attendant threw my sack down and leaped over a guardrail, almost knocking down my daughter standing in his path. He ran in hot pursuit of the young man, who was speeding on foot toward the parking lot.

The chase lasted only a few moments. We stood in the doorway, stunned, watching and listening to the man's yells of "I didn't do anything! I didn't do anything!" The young man struggled wildly, however, and we feared a bloody scene when we saw the attendant flip him over a car in order to subdue him.

We finally gained our composure, and the pursuer gained control of the young man, so we quickly walked on in. As we looked back, however, the two reentered the building still struggling and were about three steps behind us at every aisle where we turned. I yanked my daughters out of the path and the two passed on hurriedly to the store office. My daughters stared, wide-eyed, their mouths gaping in shock.

My youngest asked me later what happened, so I told her the man was probably shoplifting. "What do you mean?" she asked blankly.

"He took something out of the store without paying for it."

Her eyes widened even further, but she said nothing else.

We later discovered the man had been switching prices on merchandise, but we never found out all the details. I know one thing for sure. If my girls or any other youngsters watching that incident ever had any thoughts of shoplifting, they may have quickly changed their minds. Two normally talkative kids were remarkably silent in the car on the way home that day.

Teaching children right from wrong is a God-given responsibility for moms. We know if children are "left to themselves," they "disgrace their mother" (Proverbs 29:15). Our kids may tune us out at times, but when God unveils a life lesson in front of them, the results can be powerful — and lasting. At those times you may not need to say anything. The picture speaks for itself.

Every moment of every day is a teachable moment.

But be ready. Every moment of every day is a teachable moment. Your world — and your children's — is filled with visual, teachable opportunities. Negative images and subtle messages bombard them from the internet, television, and even friends. It's impossible to protect our kids from everything, so we need to plead for God's protection and cover them daily with our prayers also. But whether your children ever admit it or not, they are silently begging for parents who care enough to take God at his Word. They really *don't* want to be left to themselves. They've seen the results of that up close and personal.

The next time you see a teachable opportunity, seize it. God will give you wisdom. The truth is, with moms, school is never out.

DAY-BREAK

What "visual" lessons has God shown you and your children lately? When do you find the most teachable moments?

DAY-BRIEF

When God is our teacher, the truth is always clear.

DAY-VOTEDLY YOURS

Jesus, thank you for the precious opportunity to teach my children more about you. Make every day a teachable moment for us, so we can learn the lessons you spell out for us so clearly.

day 24
investments for life

It will be like a man going on a journey, who called his servants
and entrusted his wealth to them. To one he gave five bags
of gold, to another two bags, and to another one bag,
each according to his ability.
Matthew 25:14 – 15

"I'll be in first grade, and I can't read yet! Everyone else will know how, and I won't!" complained my younger daughter in frustration the week before school started.

"But, honey, that's why you're going to school," I tried to reassure her. "None of your friends read very much yet either. You'll be learning how this year."

My older daughter experienced the same frustrations whenever she sat down to her piano lesson. I think she probably expected to play like Van Cliburn after the first few lessons. (Okay, maybe not Van Cliburn, but she definitely set high expectations for herself.)

Because of prekindergarten programs and sophisticated learning gadgets, your kids may start reading and mastering basic skills much earlier than you did. But at times we're all guilty of raising the bar for achievements too high.

Sometimes we elevate those goals and expectations of ourselves and our kids because we feel it's the divine thing to do.

Society — and sometimes even parents — unknowingly drum "excellence" into our brains. Even Christian teaching can leave us confused: "If you don't use it [to the max, implied], you lose it!" That may be true especially for the "five-talent" woman. She hears that and reasons, "God gave me all these abilities. I *must* give 100 percent to each one!"

God gives all of us moms different abilities to use for him. Like the parable in Matthew 25, the steward entrusts his golden gifts to his servants: to one he gives five bags of gold, another two, and still another only one bag.

Aren't we to do our work with excellence, "with all our might" (Ecclesiastes 9:10)? To set the bar any less than one hundred percent is not … spiritual, is it? While I agree with the first statement, I've always had difficulty with the latter one. First of all, who sets the bar: God or us? Who does the work? God or us? And tell me, how can you give one hundred percent to *every* activity and *every* priority in your life — when you only have one hundred to start with?

We look around at other women who seem to pull it off. We're still trying to weigh and identify our bags of gold, but they're the speed-readers and the high achievers. Everything they touch turns to gold.

However, I've seen multigifted women crash and burn because they insist on nothing less than one hundred percent — from themselves and from others. If they offer less, they picture their destiny like the lazy servant who draws God's anger upon his return. But the principle in this passage is not about impossible standards; it's about faithfulness and stewardship. It's not about the percentage *rate* of interest return as much as it is the willingness to invest, period. It's about faith, not fear. It's about your entire life. The master would have been satisfied if the one-talent servant had simply opened a savings account and earned *some* interest on his gift. But the servant pictured the master as hard-hearted and impossible to please, rather than a generous giver who wanted to share his wealth. So he buried his gold.

But whether you consider yourself as a mega-talent or a one-talent woman, you may still struggle with this concept. Too many women see their motherhood as a roadblock to their potential. To them, stewardship of talents equates a paycheck. How can they return an interest for God when they're not even earning an income to invest? If they're not using their gifts professionally, aren't they burying them like the lazy, fearful servant?

> **God doesn't view your worth as a mom
> and a woman in dollars and cents.**

God doesn't view your worth as a mom and a woman in dollars and cents. He never has, and he never will. It took me a long time to realize that not every door that opened was God's plan for my family and me. God gave me many interests, and through the years, I've been able to dabble and even develop some of those into gifts. But only the investment of writing has brought a monetary return — and there were lean years when not even that avenue brought in a paycheck.

Did God remove the other gifts? No, I still invested them in other places: through volunteer church work, in creative ways through my children and in my home, and in the lives of others through discipleship, mentoring, or friendship. Hebrews 13:20–21 says, "May the God of peace ... equip you with everything good for doing his will, and may he work in us what is pleasing to him."

Did I invest my "gold" wisely? I hope so. As a mom, my grown children are some of the best "returns" I have. They are worth their weight in gold. But the 100 percent comes not in my equal development or investment of gifts. It's in giving them *all* to God and saying, "These 'bags' are all yours, God. Teach me where, how, and when to invest them. I trust you to work in me and bring the return you want. *Your* paycheck is enough for me! Your 'well done' is all I need."

When God sees that attitude of faith, it pleases the Master. And no amount of gold can compare to that!

DAY-BREAK

Do you consider yourself a one-bag, two-bag, or five-bag of gold woman? How have you invested what God has given you? How have some of your investments returned more than money?

DAY-BRIEF

Our children will always be good investments.

DAY-VOTEDLY YOURS

Lord, everything I have belongs to you. As your servant, help me to invest wisely whatever you give to me, so it will honor you. Use my "gold" to bless others. I live for your "well done."

day 25
creative legacies

A wise teacher makes learning a joy.
Proverbs 15:2 (LB)

One of the fond memories we moms enjoy — and carry with us from childhood — is a visit to the zoo. One of my favorite animals was the otter. The mother otter truly masters the art of creativity, in making learning a joy.

After an otter has pups, she must teach them to swim in order for them to survive and forage for their own food. Mom places her pups on dry land to play, nudging them closer and closer to the water. After a while, they ride, fearfully clinging to her back, as she ventures into the water. After several exposures to the water, the mom then begins to swim deeper, easing out from under the pups, and then swooping back under them after several minutes. Through play, they are learning how to swim, and eventually how to catch fish. One look at the otters in the zoo, and it's obvious they enjoy their "work." The mother's creativity paid off.

Motivating our children to complete their chores can be a constant battle. I decided early on to try to teach my young daughters the lesson of the otter: that creativity could make working — and learning — fun. Sounds sneaky, I know. But I really did believe that. How would I convince *them*?

I settled on a creative approach by using the skills God had given me. I drew up a treasure hunt for them. First, I wrote down some instructions in simple, poetic rhymes. One clue might read something like this:

Fold the towels, nice and straight;
Hurry now! Or you'll be late!
Place them in the bathroom too.
Behind the door you'll find the next clue!

A little corny, maybe, but the kids didn't mind. Each child received different jobs. Each clue led to another chore and the next clue in the treasure hunt. When the girls completed all their work, they found the "treasure" — usually a coupon for a special treat like an ice cream cone or a trip to the city pool.

Creativity can make working — and learning — fun.

Most of the time the girls completed their jobs without complaint. They seemed to enjoy this fun, creative approach, especially the "treasure" at the end. That lasted for a while at least.

But I never knew the rest of the story — not until a few years ago. My older daughter, now grown, confessed that she had used a little "creativity" of her own. Apparently she had tricked her younger sister into doing her jobs too by designing her own "treasure hunts." And her sweet compliant sister didn't catch on for a long time.

Apparently, though, that truth I wanted to teach them stuck, as both grown daughters moved into the field of education, using their creativity in numerous ways. Later, I was not at all surprised when both chose to become Creative Memories® (scrapbooking) consultants. They now teach other women the same joys they've discovered in their work — through their own pictorial life stories in scrapbooks. Even though distance separates their relationship by hundreds of miles, they often spend endless hours on the phone sharing and comparing the new, creative ideas they've just learned.

I guess in a way what they love doing now is helping women learn the joy of creatively designing their own legacies. Each mounted picture and written story in the women's scrapbooks is like a clue to finding buried treasure. And when each "story" is completed, at the end is a wonderful treat for their children and children's children: a treasured, creative legacy of how God has filled their lives with joy for their own unique journeys.

Creativity can make working — and learning — fun. Like the otter, maybe my creativity paid off too.

DAY-BREAK

What family memories are you preserving? What stories can you and your children and family members share? How are you making learning a joy for your children?

DAY-BRIEF

God-stories — are good stories.

DAY-VOTEDLY YOURS

Lord, thank you for being a creative God and for making me unique. Help me to be a wise teacher, guiding my children with creativity, joy, and purpose.

day 26
knee prints

Each one had a harp and they were holding golden bowls
full of incense, which are the prayers of God's people.
Revelation 5:8

"Mom, you need some new carpet in my old bedroom! Some places near my bed are really getting faded and worn!"

The mom just smiled and nodded. Her adult prodigal had just returned for a short visit. Still living in rebellion, he was softening and had decided to at least stop by "just to say hello." She knew about those worn places. She wasn't about to change the carpet. She just called those her "knee prints," because they represented years of pleas to God on behalf of her wayward son.

Maybe you can identify with that mom. You read all the parenting books (well, at least a few of the 75,000 currently available ones). You committed your child to God before his birth. You enrolled him in the church nursery at six weeks old. You even sent him to a Christian school. You taught him the right values, and cautioned him against wrong friendships. He knew how to make right choices. You loved him as only a mother could love her son. So what went wrong?

I'm sure Manoah's wife may have asked the same questions of her son, Samson. He was a miracle child from birth — a son promised to her by an angel of the Lord. Scripture doesn't say she *asked* for a son — and after raising Samson, we moms may wonder if she ever entertained thoughts of, "Why *did* you give us this son, God?"

However, the angel gave Manoah's wife a set of strict instructions: "From his very conception, treat him as a Nazirite — no haircuts, no drinking wine or eating fruit of the grapevine, no touching dead bodies" (cf. Judges 13:5; also Numbers 6:2 – 8). Normally a voluntary, and often temporary, vow of "separation," these instructions regarding Samson were for life. After she told her husband about the angel's visit, Manoah asked for the instructions again, so he could hear it for himself. They wanted to get this parenting thing right. So the angel of God visited again and reiterated his first words. After the angel left, the couple realized they had been in the presence of God and fell on their faces.

It was probably not the last time they fell to their knees, face-down to the floor — but not for the same reason as before. Samson was a model son, blessed by God, until he turned eighteen — or whenever he decided it was time to pick a wife. He returned home one day after playing the field in Philistine territory and demanded that his parents get him a Philistine woman he had seen as his wife. Mom and Dad tried to reason with him, but Samson insisted: "Get her for me. She's the right one for me" (Judges 14:3).

Little did Samson know that his poor choice was the beginning of the end. In spite of his superhuman, God-given strength, Samson had obvious weaknesses — not only for women. He rebelled against his parents, was deceitful, had temper tantrums, sought out a prostitute, was filled with pride, and broke his Nazirite vow, just to name a few.

But behind the scenes, Mom didn't know that God was still at work in Samson's life. She didn't realize that God planned to override their son's foolishness and use him to destroy some of the Philistines' stranglehold on Israel. It was his design from the beginning, and God does not abandon his purposes. Deceived by a woman named Delilah, Samson was shaved, captured by his enemy, robbed of his sight, and spent the remainder of his life grinding grain.

But in his dying moments, when his hair had grown long again, Samson cried out to God, and God heard him. Wrapping huge arms around the Philistine temple pillars, Samson pulled the entire structure down — on himself and scores of Philistines. Minutes before he died, Samson, the broken prodigal, had returned "home."

The last scene we see is a sad picture of Samson's brothers and his father's entire family coming to bury him (see Judges 13 – 16).

The Bible doesn't tell us how Samson's mom dealt with her son's wild rebelliousness during his adult years. I think it's safe to say she probably left lots of "knee prints" on the floor beside his bed.

And so can we. If you're struggling with a rebellious child, accept that some battles are not yours, but God's. He may not set your child apart to lead a nation or confront a dangerous enemy, but he creates every child with a unique purpose in mind.

God knows what to do to bring your child home.

God is always at work in our children's lives. Samson's mom did her part. Then God did his. Just as he kept his hand on Samson, he will not let go of your child. If you find in spite of everything that your resolve and your faith are slipping away, hold on to Jesus. Join an army of other mothers who are leaving eternal "knee prints" on the carpet throughout their homes — for their grown children and for the ones still at home. Gather with other moms to cry out for the life of your child, consistently. If it had not been for God's grace, you could have been that child yourself — and maybe you were.

Remember that God never gave up on you and never stopped loving you, and he is still in control. Pray that your child will come to himself, like Samson, even to the *end* of himself, if that's what it takes. God knows what to do to bring your child home. He wants you to keep believing and to keep resting in him.

I like to think that one day when you get to heaven, there will be an unmistakable aroma wafting through the air, sweeter than the sweetest perfume imaginable. And as you're standing there, wondering what it is, Jesus takes your hand and tells you that perfume was made from the prayers of God's people ascending toward heaven.

I would venture to say that that aroma included scores of prayers from moms just like you, who wore out the carpet with their tears and their "knee prints."

DAY-BREAK

Have you or someone you know ever struggled with a prodigal

child? What did you do? If that child is yours, reaffirm your faith and your resolve to hold on to Jesus and to keep leaving as many knee prints on the carpet as are necessary.

DAY-BRIEF

When in doubt, faith it out with God.

DAY-VOTEDLY YOURS

Lord, keep my children on the right path. Turn their hearts toward you and never let them stray too far. I trust my children — at home and grown — into your keeping, Lord. It's the safest place I know.

extravagant love

But God demonstrates his own love for us in this:
While we were still sinners, Christ died for us.
Romans 5:8

Much of my husband's childhood years were spent on a lake in West Texas where his parents and grandparents owned a fishing camp. Like all boys, Larry loved to play "buried treasure." The sand around the camp offered multiple opportunities for realistic pirating adventures.

But one fateful day, Larry learned a powerful lesson he never forgot. Here's his story:

"At the fishing camp, people were always coming and going: stocking up on groceries, searching out the best fishing lures, and renting campsites nearby to set up tents. Mom kept a small file box in the house in which she saved silver dollars. One day I spied that box and saw 'Capt. Kidd' and 'Treasure' written all over it. I opened it up and counted fifty shiny coins — not much in today's economy, but a huge sum to my parents in those days — and definitely a realistic treasure for a pirate. I thought it would be cool to 'bury' that treasure box, so I took it out to an empty tent behind our house where I was playing with some other kids. We had great fun pretending we were burying our treasure inside that tent.

"But as boys often do, I got distracted and forgot about the box of silver dollars. Two or three days later, Mom asked about the box. Suddenly I remembered that I had left them in the tent. So I hurried out back, confident I would be the pirate hero and retrieve the buried treasure for the 'damsel in distress.'

"But when I looked in the tent, there was no box. I pawed through every corner as sand flew in every direction. No box. No treasure. No silver dollars. And *no* pirate hero. I returned to face my fate from a mom who was now *greatly* 'in distress.'

"I'll never forget my mother's words. She didn't punish me. She didn't chew me out. She didn't take away my fishing or pirating privileges. She said two things that left a dramatic impression on me. With obvious disappointment, she said, 'We could have fed our family for a month with that money.' She let her words hang in the air for a moment, then reached out to hug me. Then she said, 'But I forgive you.'

"An enemy pirate couldn't have sliced me any deeper. Another 'pirate' had obviously stolen the treasure, but the responsibility lay directly in my hands."

> **Through a mom's forgiveness, she has
> the divine opportunity to model Christ's own
> forgiveness to her children.**

Through a mom's forgiveness, she has the divine opportunity to model Christ's own love to her children.

Badgering, abusing, screaming, berating — these are not

God's tools. They're more like "enemy" pirate behavior. Certainly, appropriate discipline is needed when outright disobedience challenges parental authority. But Larry's mom wisely understood how to drive home the consequences of a boy's foolish mistake and childish behavior without wounding his character. Her words stung and made him realize the extreme carelessness of his actions. But it was his mom's forgiveness that taught him the most about extravagant love.

Only God can teach that kind of love. He *is* extravagant love, personified. Almost two thousand years ago, he saw the extreme "pirating" of his world. The ones he created didn't understand their true purpose and instead chose their own way through sinful behavior. The cost to God was overwhelming. He knew the ultimate consequences of sin. He didn't excuse it. But he took his most extravagant, expensive treasure — his own Son — and offered it as a gift to his world in distress. And with a holy whisper of grace, he said, "What you've done is not acceptable. But I forgive you."

And those who still hear him and receive his extravagant love and forgiveness will never forget it. They will never be the same again.

DAY-BREAK

In what ways did your mom show you extravagant love? How have you demonstrated forgiveness to your own children? How has God shown that kind of love and forgiveness to you?

DAY-BRIEF

Forgiveness is not always easy, but it is always right.

DAY-VOTEDLY YOURS

Father, what an awesome God you are! Thank you for your extravagant love and forgiveness. Teach me to model that kind of love to my children, so they can see Jesus clearly in me.

day 28

true greatness

Unless you change and become like little children,
you will never enter the kingdom of heaven. Therefore,
whoever takes a humble place — becoming like this child
— is the greatest in the kingdom of heaven.
Matthew 18:3 – 4

A young servant girl captured by a band of Syrian raiders heard that her new master, a commander in the Syrian army, had leprosy. In a spirit of revenge, she could have remained silent. But her faith — and her God — were too real to let pride persuade her otherwise. She boldly offered a solution: "If only my master would see the prophet who is in Samaria! He would cure him of his leprosy" (2 Kings 5:3).

The little girl didn't say *maybe*. Her declaration smacked of genuine belief in a God who worked through prophets like Elisha. Her childlike faith followed her into enemy territory, and she couldn't be quiet about this precious commodity.

But when Naaman came to see Elisha and heard the prescription for healing from Elisha's servant, it wasn't what he was expecting: "Go, wash yourself seven times in the Jordan, and your flesh will be restored and you will be cleansed" (2 Kings 5:10).

Naaman's pride surged, and he turned away in rage at such a

ridiculous suggestion. Perhaps he wanted something a little more suited to his rank. His servant boldly said, "If the prophet had told you to do some great thing, would you not have done it?" (2 Kings 5:13). But Elisha knew his request would mean a humbling of Naaman's proud heart. So Naaman dipped himself seven times just as Elisha said, and his flesh was like a little child's again!

And apparently, so was his faith. This time Naaman stood face-to-face with Elisha and confessed his new, childlike faith in the God of Israel. He even wanted to take two mule loads of Israel's dirt back to his land so he could offer true sacrifices to his new God on Israelite soil (2 Kings 5:17 – 19).

Jesus talked about that kind of humble faith when his disciples were dealing with their own pride issue. They asked Jesus, "Who, then, is the greatest in the kingdom of heaven?" (Matthew 18:1).

But his answer was not what they expected. He called a small child over to him and used that child as an object lesson. But what did he mean by "change and become like little children"? Jesus went on to explain. Most people boast of greatness in terms of success, wealth, and rank — maybe like the army commander Naaman. Maybe the disciples even thought of themselves as great and wanted to inherit the "best place" in God's kingdom.

But God's kingdom will not house prideful tenants. The ones who actually live there — and in God's eyes, they will *all* be great — are those who have emptied themselves of selfish motives and boastful living, those whose hearts are as humble and faith-filled as little children.

Our greatest task is to help our children
understand what it means to be "great"
in the kingdom of God.

It's the kind of faith you want to see — and maybe already have seen — in the lives of your children. Some of you moms would even admit that God used your own child to bring *you* to Jesus, the Healer of body, mind, and soul.

Children's hearts are soft and pliable in their early years and not seasoned with cynicism and pride. That means your godly influence on your children can make a huge difference then. We may encourage our kids to be "great" in many areas — music, science, the arts, and sports. But our greatest task is to help them understand what it means to be "great" in the kingdom of God. If they miss that, nothing else matters.

Teach them about Jesus early. If you are still raising young children, nourish their spiritual appetite as soon as their questions begin. Ungodly influences are ready to capture our kids' hearts and minds in both subtle and overt ways the second they pass through the birth canal.

As a mom, make God a household word. Let them know that Jesus is not an unseen guest in your home; he is a permanent resident who is felt, heard, and seen with eyes of faith. Keep on praying for God to keep their hearts humble and their faith real (yours too) so that when the opportunity comes, they will be generous in sharing it boldly.

Jesus was illustrating a different point altogether in Luke 4:24, but he spoke about the times in which Naaman — and Elisha — lived. Jesus said many had leprosy then, but only one was healed — Naaman. And God used the faith of a humble child to bring that about.

As moms we have the opportunity to both learn and demonstrate true "greatness" when we're willing to humble ourselves like little children.

It's one of the greatest gifts we can give our kids.

DAY-BREAK

Who first taught you about Jesus and childlike faith? How are you teaching your children about true greatness in God's kingdom?

DAY-BRIEF

We cannot *lead* our children to a place we've never been.

DAY-VOTEDLY YOURS

Lord, what a beautiful privilege you have given me as a mom to teach my children about you. Keep my heart like that of a little child, so I can model the kind of faith they too need to embrace.

the great escape

Oh, that I had the wings of a dove!
    I would fly away and be at rest.
I would flee far away
    and stay in the desert.

Psalm 55:6 – 7

I looked outside wistfully at the birds gathering in my backyard one morning. A dove lighted on a leafy tree branch and then flew away.

"That's me! I just need to get away!" I cried out to the Lord in a sudden burst of emotion. The mounting pressures of motherhood, ministry, and PMS (it was so bad, I used to call it "pre-monster syndrome") left me drained emotionally, spiritually, and physically. So I ran away.

Don't worry. It was only for a day — five or six hours at the most. But I needed to regroup, rethink, recharge, and rest. A nearby park with a lake offered a welcome invitation. I grabbed my Bible, notebook, and pen and headed out the door. The children wouldn't be home from school for several hours, and I could call my husband to let him know of my plan.

All of us moms feel the responsibilities of life and motherhood closing in on us at times, threatening to clip our wings and ground us in exhaustion. Maybe you too have longed for the wings

of a dove so you could fly away from those pressures, if even for a
short while.

My husband and I learned through the years how important it
was to create those needed "retreats" for ourselves and even for each
other as a couple. One of our favorite places to escape yearly took
us to the beach, where the rhythmic waves of the ocean soothed our
spirits. Exchanging turns with friends or family to keep children,
we enjoyed "flying away" to remove pressure and restore energy with
rest and relaxation. There's something about water, whether a lake
or ocean, that renews the soul. David the psalmist wrote of its pro-
found effect on his life in the familiar twenty-third psalm: "He leads
me beside quiet waters, he refreshes my soul" (Psalm 23:2 – 3).

> *God reminds me that deep inside me, underneath*
> *the crashing turmoil and waves of pressure,*
> *is a peace and calm, a quiet place*
> *to which I can retreat, again and again.*

But one year I learned a strange truth about the ocean. To
the casual onlooker, the ocean might not appear as a calm retreat.
But deep underneath the crashing turmoil of its mounting waves
along the bottom — away from all the activity — is a peace and
calm where none of the water is disturbed.

My trips always brought me refreshment, but how I longed to
remain in that calm, unruffled state with no pressures, no challenges, and no conflicts. While our bodies and spirits may need
to hide away and escape at times, the call of responsibility always
beckons us home. Even the dove mama's "rest" is short-lived.

Imagine the time she spends building a nest, laying her eggs, feeding her young, and starting the process all over again.

Life is not a constant retreat. Our getaways are, at best, temporary. Or are they?

There is no need to "run away" anymore as I did that day as a young mom. I no longer depend on those kinds of flights for my emotional or spiritual survival. God reminds me often that deep inside me, underneath the crashing turmoil and waves of pressure, is a peace and calm, a quiet place to which I can retreat, again and again.

When I am still and truly listen, I can hear the voice of Jesus whispering, "Come to me, all you who are weary and burdened, and I will give you rest" (Matthew 11:28). He offers that to all of us moms.

That's a "getaway" invitation I can't resist.

DAY-BREAK

When have you wanted to "fly away and be at rest"? What did you do to handle those feelings? What are your favorite kinds of retreats?

DAY-BRIEF

You can never "get away" from God.

DAY-VOTEDLY YOURS

God, I am so much in need of your rest! The next time I am tempted to "fly away," help me to run to you for renewal and restoration.

behind closed doors

*No temptation has overtaken you except what is common
to us all. And God is faithful; he will not let you be tempted
beyond what you can bear. But when you are tempted, he will
also provide a way out so that you can endure it.*
1 Corinthians 10:13

When my children were only toddlers, they loved to head for open doors the moment they waddled out of bed. I had to move faster than they did to close the doors before they "got into something." One day they decided to "bathe" in the commode, taste Mom's cologne, and play dress-up with my makeup, while another day they collided with dresser mirrors, painted the drawers and walls with lipstick, and poured out a perfectly good bottle of shampoo.

In big sister's room, the younger one usually grabbed the marking pens, Crayolas, and glue — and of course, anything small enough to deposit in her mouth, including a wad of gum from the wastebasket. Sometimes when I closed the door just before they entered, they would react with toddler tantrums, beating their hands or feet against the door in angry protests.

Curiosity is a natural part of a child's life, and temptation often takes them to dangerous places. No matter how many safety locks, caps, or gates we use, our kids will sometimes find an opening.

That happened to us one day when our oldest managed to squeeze through the door to Larry's workshop area. We had been refinishing some furniture earlier and had left a small cup of turpentine sitting on the shelf, barely within reach of her tiny fingers. We were both in the yard, thinking the other was watching our daughter. But when I found our toddler, she was standing next to the shelf, the cup of flammable liquid on the floor near her. I detected the strong odor and immediately checked her mouth.

The telltale smell of lingering turpentine on her breath sent us into a tailspin, and we rushed her to the local hospital emergency room. Apparently she ingested none of the dangerous liquid, and probably only touched the cup to her mouth, but it scared us badly.

As they grow older, we can no longer close doors *ahead* of our kids. But we spend a lot of time closing the ones they leave standing open (to hide teen clutter). They make their own choices, but we still help them out when they open the wrong doors (it's called grounding). Hopefully, by the time they're young adults, they've learned *some* doors need to stay closed, often through their own painful experiences.

> *God knows what can happen "behind closed doors,"*
> *so he often shuts them for our benefit —*
> *before we try to slip past them.*

But what about moms? "I'm an adult," you say. "I'm free to walk through any door I want." Unfortunately, temptation has no age limit. You may *think* you can handle a potentially volatile situation, but God knows your fallibility. Divorce courts are filled with moms whose marriages and families dissolved into flames. They *thought* they could handle substance abuse or a simple "adjustment" in their company's financial records. They *thought* they could put a cap on their anger or hide an unpaid store item in their purse. They *thought* they could handle a harmless computer chat room or an occasional office "date" as long as the fire stayed under control.

And while you may only crack the door open a little, your child — or teen — may throw the same door wide open. Act wisely. Your children are watching. Your family's future welfare may hang in the balance.

God is watching you too. Instead of seeing that as a negative trait about your heavenly Father, thank him profusely that he is both omniscient and omnipresent: he is the epitome of wisdom and he is everywhere. You can never get away from him! God knows what can happen "behind closed doors," so he often shuts them for our benefit — before we try to slip past them. You may not understand why, and you may be tempted to get angry with God. But in time, we often discover his reason was the same as we had for our toddlers or teens — for our protection.

We moms can not only help our children respect God's — and our own parental — "closed doors," but we can encourage each other as women as well. Instead of isolating yourself, seek out Christian friends who can keep you accountable. Ask them to pray for you and your family, especially when you sense the strong pull of a wrong temptation.

Temptation will come to all of us, and no one is strong enough to handle it alone. It will often look like a harmless open door. But before you head through that opening, remember God will make a way out for you. He will shut all other doors, except the one through which you can escape.

And when you enter that one, he'll shut it tightly behind you. Behind his door there is nothing but safety.

DAY-BREAK

What doors have your children tried to open through the years? How has God helped you through times of temptation?

DAY-BRIEF

When God says, "Do not enter," there's always a good reason.

DAY-VOTEDLY YOURS

Jesus, you are my door of safety, and I'm so glad you're watching over my family and me. Give us wisdom to discern wrong temptations, and surround us constantly with yourself and your love.

desperate moms

Daughter, your faith has healed you. Go in peace.
Luke 8:48

She eased into the crowd slowly, carefully, so she wouldn't attract attention. Surely no one would notice her. But as soon as she found a place, the press of the crowd swept her along like a dead branch in a surging stream. Her thoughts were frantic and choppy. *I must ... get to ... him.* What little energy her body could muster was slowly ebbing away. *He ... is ... my only ... hope. If I could just ... touch his garment ...* She was desperate.

Jesus was her last shred of hope. For twelve years she had endured hemorrhaging with no cure. Doctors couldn't help; women shunned her. She'd spent everything she had. She lived like a social outcast, and she felt so alone. And she could feel the life draining from her body, mind, and spirit. But she had heard about this man called Jesus, a miracle worker.

Suddenly the crowd slowed a moment, and then stopped. She peeked around the couple in front of her, catching a glimpse of Jesus' robe. He was talking to someone — a man. She almost lost her balance, as the crush of people started moving again. The woman spied an opening and moved in closer. As she did so, she reached out in desperation. *Just a few ... more ... steps!* Suddenly she lunged with every ounce of strength left in her, as one hand grabbed the hem of Jesus' outer cloak.

Jesus stopped. Startled, the woman turned to make her escape, but the crowd was too dense. Jesus' words caught her off guard: "Who touched me?... Power has gone out from me" (Luke 8:45 – 46).

The woman was trapped, imprisoned by the mob surrounding her, so she fell at Jesus' feet and poured out her story. Immediately, Jesus rewarded her faith with healing. She was a new woman, free — free to go in peace! (Luke 8:40 – 48).

Maybe that's you. A "crowd" of unexpected circumstances are pressing in, all around you. You feel hopeless, caught between the heavy responsibilities of motherhood and marriage, or a mountain of urgent deadlines. At times you may feel as if you can't drag out of bed one more morning. You are desperate for God's intervention.

With one hand, you can hold onto theirs; with the other, you can hold on to the edge of Jesus' garment for them.

Or perhaps it's someone you know. You see them everywhere, imprisoned behind invisible walls in your own church and neighborhood. They wear plastic smiles to cover a shell of a soul. They answer, "Fine," when you inquire, but they're dying inside. Their elementary school child is already on drugs; their teen is pregnant and unmarried, and they've turned in desperation to the drink that numbs their exhausted minds and bodies. You see them harried and single, depositing their little ones at daycare as they speed to a job interview with a cell phone in one hand and a tube of lipstick in the other. If this job doesn't pan out …

Or maybe you've noticed them in Bible study, plastered with too-heavy makeup, a futile attempt to cover up the purplish-yellow bruises on their faces. They are the silent victims on your church roll. The husband is a model leader, but no one knows … except the children — and they are too scared to tell.

They're trying to hold everything together without falling apart, but they are on their last shred of hope. They are longing for something, anything, someone to fill the gaping holes in their souls.

And just like the woman with the hemorrhage, they want to reach out. They may be different ages, but they have two things in common. They are moms — and they are women who are desperate.

If you ask, God will bring them across your path. Don't worry. You won't have to fight the press of the crowd. They usually walk alone. But you have something they need. Maybe you've walked there too, maybe not. But to some women, you may be their only hope. With one hand, you can hold onto theirs; with the other, you can hold on to the edge of Jesus' garment for them — because too many of them no longer have the strength to reach that far.

Moms — and women — need each other. Remember what it was like to be desperate for God. Then show someone the way to hope again.

And if that someone is you, Jesus knows your heart. And he wants to grant healing and peace to you too.

DAY-BREAK

When have you felt desperate for God? Think about other moms and women who may be struggling with similar feelings. Pray for them by name, and ask God to help you show them the way to find peace, joy, and hope again.

DAY-BRIEF

One step of faith can mean the difference between desperation — and hope.

DAY-VOTEDLY YOURS

Lord, I know what it's like in the tunnel of despair. But you have shown me the light. You have restored my joy. Help me to show others the way out too.

day 32
forever flowers

Now he who supplies seed to the sower and bread for food
will also supply and increase your store of seed and will
enlarge the harvest of your righteousness.
2 Corinthians 9:10

Anne walked through her garden, hoping to gather enough blooms for at least one more floral bouquet. The growing season was almost past, and she hated to see the dead, skeletal remains of spent flowers, awaiting their ultimate destiny. She knew little about gardening, but this was her first real attempt, and she had tended her garden carefully, planting a variety of pretty colors.

Was it worth all the trouble for just a few days of brilliant color? Next year, she'd have to start all over again — buying expensive new plants. Then there was the planning, seeding, watering, feeding. *A lot of work!*

When she finished snipping and sorting, Anne lifted the mixed assortment of colorful flowers to her nose, inhaling the faint fragrance of nature's natural perfume. *Ah!* Laying the bouquet aside for a moment, she took her scissors and reluctantly cut away the useless "deadheads," her favorite term for the lifeless flower stubs in the garden. Some of the petals had fallen to the ground earlier and lay broken and crushed, leaving a carpet of fading color.

Anne reached for her plastic garbage bag and grabbed a handful of dead flowers she had cut for disposal. But as she did, she noticed a shower of tiny fragments falling from some of the plants down to the ground. She sifted through them, and to her great delight she discovered seeds. *Hum.* Instead of throwing them out, Anne had a better idea. She ran back into the house for a Ziplock bag and dropped a few of the seeds inside it. Then she looked down at the garden soil. *Why not?* She loosened the dirt around the stems, and with a metal trowel, she began scattering the seeds, pushing the remainder of them, still on the ground, further into the soil.

Anne was involved in a car accident the following winter. An extended recuperation followed, and her days were filled with rehabilitation. Her husband and kids stepped in to help, but none of them had the time or inclination for gardening. The doctor told her that even simple tasks like working in her garden would bring extreme pain because of the extent of her injuries.

The next spring, Anne couldn't plant new flowers. She would miss the fragrance that once filled her home. One day in late April she managed enough strength to hobble outside to the garden she had left dormant. Expecting to see a naked mound of dirt or a pile of weeds, Anne gasped in surprise. Before her stood a color-ful array of fresh, new flower buds covering the garden — red, yel-low, blue, and orange. *What in the world?* A few plants had pushed through the ground where she had "replanted" the seeds the year before. *It worked!* But what about the others? Did someone sneak into her garden and plant some flowers when she was unaware?

Anne had not taken the time to research the "right" plants for her area or season last year. She didn't even know all that she had planted. They had just looked pretty, and she liked their color and fragrance. But now she had some time. When she had finished browsing online and through a faded garden magazine her mom had given her years earlier, she identified the flowers in her garden. Most of them were "perennial." She laughed out loud as she paraphrased her findings: *When nature cooperates, they are like "forever flowers," returning, every year!*

Anne looked into her closet where she had placed the forgotten seeds she'd bagged last year. An idea began to form. *Tomorrow, I need to give some seeds away!*

God is the Master Gardener. And his lessons are worth learning, if you'll do the research.

Maybe you feel like that mom. For whatever reason, the fragrance of your life has faded. You've tried to make a difference, but nothing seems to last. Your life is like a spent flower, and like those stubby plants, you feel destined for an early graveyard. You remember the faint aroma as you presented your own special fragrance to God. You thought he wanted to use you in colorful ways, but now you're really wondering. The opportunities don't seem to knock on your door as before. You try to sift through the crushed petals and the faded memories of days when God seemed real, and you were touching women's lives. You think to yourself, *If I am to be a sweet aroma to God, where is the perfume?*

But God is the Master Gardener. And his lessons are worth learning, if you'll do the research. You plant the seeds, but he brings the growth. The sweetest perfume often comes from the flowers that have been crushed and broken. His care for you is not only perennial; it's forever — and he is always mixing new fragrances for your life. He snips and prunes the useless stubs from our lives in order to make us more productive.

And what about the seeds that fell from your life and were buried, out of sight and mind? Your children, your friends, your neighbors, the places you scattered his truths? The seeds you bagged and gave away? Those flowers are springing up all around you, forming a beautiful bouquet. You may not see them yet, but God does. He is taking your sacrifices and your hard work and is turning them into a fragrant offering.

So the next time you think your gardening days are over, remember Anne — and the lessons from the Master Gardener. You are God's "forever flower." He isn't finished with you yet.

DAY-BREAK

What's blooming in your garden? What seeds have you planted? If you haven't tried before, start a garden this year. Pick a small plot, and ask your children to help. Then teach them the lessons from the Master Gardener.

DAY-BRIEF

God selects the fragrance; we scatter the seeds.

DAY-VOTEDLY YOURS

Lord, thank you for the truths you so patiently teach me. Forgive me when I become discouraged or forget that you are always at work, even when I can't see or sense it. You are the fragrance of my life!

day 33
pause to refresh

I will refresh the weary and satisfy the faint.
Jeremiah 31:25

"I'm just taking a break! I only stopped work for a second!"

Betty's husband had left work early and just walked into the bedroom, where he found her sprawled on top of the bed, reading a book.

He just shook his head and chuckled. Betty's home business had escalated, and her days had merged into nights for several weeks now. The children hadn't returned home from school yet, and Betty had taken a well-deserved break. Her husband had encouraged her to ease up a little, but Betty still drove herself too hard. Her comment obviously proved she still struggled, even when she did stop to take a breath.

Betty knew her husband was right. When she worked too hard, crankiness set in, and her children could tell the difference.

Every woman, like Betty, needs refreshing moments in her life — times she can carve out just for her alone. Even if she loves her work, a mom needs to stop and refocus now and then. The demands of motherhood — and life — can leave her depleted.

In an earlier devotion you read about "pray dates," a special time for reconnection with God. In another one I mentioned the need for women to keep marriage intimacy alive by making time for husbands. Throughout the book, I've encouraged you to keep nourishing relationships, both horizontal (with others) and vertical (with God). Each chapter has offered you a different slant on similar themes. Do you feel sometimes like you're spinning ten plates at once, and as soon as you get the last one going, the first one needs attention again?

Personal refreshment contributes to a joyful outlook.

I don't believe God intended for us to be "dull" women — "all work and no play." Relationships do take work, and work does take time. In the same way that unruly preschoolers need occasional "time outs," so do you as a mom. Only your time out is for a different reason. Personal refreshment contributes to a joyful outlook. And others love to be around refreshed people — especially your family members.

Whether it's something major, like taking a new exercise class, starting a hobby, growing flowers in your own garden like Anne, or just carving out a few moments to curl up with a good book like Betty, pause for refreshment. Take a bubble bath. Walk around the block. Grab a second cup of coffee, or call an old girlfriend, but do something you enjoy, if possible, every day.

I keep plenty of "hobbies" handy for my own pleasure times, and I love reading great fiction. But feeling the pressure of looming deadlines, the other day I printed out some funny anecdotes from a humor file on my computer. I had never read most of them, only filed them away as soon as they appeared in my inbox on busy days. I sat down on the living room couch and browsed through all of them, enjoying my own private, fifteen-minute, laugh-out-loud laugh-in. Then I shared a few with Larry when he came home, and the belly laughs started all over again. When we finished, I felt as if I had walked through a refreshing spring shower.

Still feel like you have no flexibility? A speaker at a conference once challenged us as women to see how many things we could do in only fifteen minutes a day. I accepted that challenge and couldn't believe the enjoyable — as well as unpleasant — tasks I could accomplish in that short of time, if I would only do it. A fifteen-minute time slot may not seem very long, but it's the actual *pause* that refreshes, not the amount of time you spend enjoying it.

Don't be discouraged if on some days, taking time out seems impossible. Even the act of giving to others will bring refreshment to you as you learn to see life from God's perspective (Proverbs 11:25).

Remember, it's God who gives you good things to enjoy. And he loves to refresh his children.

DAY-BREAK

Do you have any hobbies? What kinds of things do you enjoy doing? What are your biggest challenges in finding some time for yourself?

DAY-BRIEF

The busiest people are not *always* the happiest.

DAY-VOTEDLY YOURS

God, you are truly the pause that refreshes me most. Help me to be wise with the time you give so I can enjoy every moment — and every relationship you give — in the way you intended.

day 34
the friendship connection

*I have called you friends, for everything that I learned
from my Father I have made known to you.*
John 15:15

I ran into her at the post office one day. We had met briefly only one other time. I asked her how she was, and she lowered her head. When she looked up at me, a lone tear trickled down her face. "I'm so lonely. I need a friend. I just feel disconnected."

Through the years, God has brought them across my path: both young women and teens to my doorstep, older women to my kitchen table, and women who were nonbelievers in some temporary office jobs. He's placed women of all ages in Bible studies I've taught.

God has given me a microphone at the podium and a platform through written encouragement — and friendships have developed as a result of both. And in recent years, as I've spent more and more time at home working at a computer, he has brought women to me through cyberspace.

Almost all of those women needed the same thing: friendship, connection, purpose. They are not all "girlfriends." Some are mere acquaintances. But in the stressful lives we have as moms, we all need those female relationships in which we don't feel compelled to impress, but with whom we can relax and "de-stress." That's what happens when women connect with other women.

You may think all good friendships are based on sameness and similarity: same age, similar interests, equal number of kids, and the like. But I've had both younger and older girlfriends. When you need "connection" through women friendships, think about these possibilities: a friend in *deed*. She's the friend who buys you a new pair of shoes when your child stops up the commode with yours, the one who keeps your baby when you're throwing up, the woman who brings you chicken soup (and chocolate) the day you come home from the hospital, and the one who cleans your shower (yuk!) when you don't have the strength to do it yourself. She's a friend who *loves* to help.

> *In the stressful lives we have as moms, we all need those female relationships in which we don't feel compelled to impress, but with whom we can relax and de-stress.*

Or there's the friend in *need*: She's the one who's waiting at the emergency room — before you even get there; the one who listens to you cry when you lose your mom. She's the woman who says with a hug, "It'll be okay," when the doctor announces, "It's cancer," and the one who holds your heart when your husband walks out on you. She's the friend you found during a crisis.

I have five women friends who *intercede* for me, for my speaking and writing ministry, for my husband and children, and for my own personal Christian growth. There are days (most of them) when I simply cry out, "God, I can't do this, but you can!" Knowing that these women and other girlfriends (and my husband!) are fervently praying for me too makes all the difference.

God may give you a friend in *creed*: one who shares the same beliefs you do and attends a women's Bible study with you; the one who shares lunch and who encourages you to keep growing in your relationship with Christ.

Or he may bring a friend into your life that's "anti-creed." She's the one whose beliefs may be unlike yours, or just opposite in personality, but she may challenge you to move beyond your normal comfort zone, sometimes even beyond the church walls to share your influence — and your God.

You may picture some kinds of relationships as "unlikely" friendships, like the one between an 8,700-pound elephant named Tarra and Bella, a small dog. In this Tennessee sanctuary of pachyderms, each "retired" elephant searches out a girlfriend, a buddy — and all have selected other elephant friendships except those two. Complete opposites, Tarra and Bella have chosen to hang out together with each other for years. When Bella sustained a spinal cord injury, she lay paralyzed for three weeks in the sanctuary office. Instead of roaming the 2,700 acres, Elephant Tarra wouldn't leave. She stood outside the office and waited for her canine friend Bella to get well.[10]

So if you're looking for connection, remember that friendships come in all sizes and shapes, and are formed in all kinds of situations, even in the Bible — like Mary and Martha as sisters; Ruth and Naomi as mother-in-law and daughter-in-law; Dorcas, with the widows she helped; or Rebekah and Deborah, her nurse.

"But I'm one of those moms with no connections," you may

be saying. "God hasn't given me *any* of those kinds of friendships. Even my female relatives live too far away."

Then I've just offered you numerous ways for you to *make* a friend. Take the initiative. The old adage "to have a friend, you must be one" is still true. The One who loves you (Jesus) calls you "friend." Tell him what you need.

Then ask him to help you *be* a friend — *indeed*.

DAY-BREAK

What kind of friendships has God brought your way in the past? If you have few women friends right now and are in need of connection, what steps will you take this week to make a friend and be a friend indeed?

DAY-BRIEF

For the most satisfying journey, the best ship is friendship.

DAY-VOTEDLY YOURS

Lord Jesus, when I think of my best friend, it's you. You are there in all the ways I need. Help me be the kind of friend to others that you are to me.

the real model

Let the little children come to me, and do not hinder them,
for the kingdom of God belongs to such as these.
Luke 18:16

Moms don't know where to find role models for their kids these days.

Confessions of steroids and drug use reveal that some of your son's sports heroes aren't so super after all. Senators or law officers admit corruption; temperamental musicians self-destruct; and even your daughter's favorite wholesome television character may pose for *Playboy* in real life. What's a mother to do?

Some moms will remember singing along with Mr. Rogers and his "Wonderful Day in the Neighborhood" song when you were a child or when your kids were small. Mr. Rogers died in 2003, but kids can still watch his videos or see reruns on public television.

Fred Rogers was a musician, a puppeteer, a children's television producer, a writer, and a Presbyterian minister — with a heart as big as Texas. At his death and all through his life, people used words like *kind, gentle, good, loving, consistent, happy, positive,* and *friendly* to describe him.

After Mr. Roger's death I spent some time journaling about

his life. People came from everywhere to thank him for his honesty. I think it was because he represented wholesomeness, innocence, and a lost virtue that children need so much.

I remember an interview with Mr. Rogers, dressed in his traditional, hand-sewn cardigan and sneakers, when he told of an adult woman who came up to him one day. The woman said when she was a little girl, she had been abused and raped, and she listened to Mr. Rogers. She said, "I believed you on TV when you sang, 'You're special.'" Mr. Rogers said something holy happened between the television screen and that little girl's hearing. It was a holy moment.

If you as a mom want a perfect role model for your child, you won't have to look any further for a "nurturing place" than the pages of God's Word.

Mr. Rogers received thirty honorary degrees and numerous awards, including the Presidential Medal of Freedom, the nation's highest civilian honor, for his "extraordinary public television programming ... his legendary commitment to young people ... and a career that demonstrates the importance of kindness, compassion, and learning."[11]

Mr. Rogers chose the avenue of television because he wanted TV to be a nurturing place for kids. At least his program did that. For thirty-five years on PBS, *Mister Rogers' Neighborhood* received every major television award, including four Emmy awards. During the 1997 Daytime Emmys, the Lifetime Achievement Award was presented to Rogers. Tom Junod in *Esquire*'s coverage of the event wrote this:

> Mister Rogers ... said into the microphone, "All of us have special ones who have loved us into being. Would you just take, along with me, ten seconds to think of the people who have helped you become who you are? Ten seconds of silence ... I'll watch the time."

The audience thought maybe he was kidding, but he wasn't. Junod wrote, "The jaws clenched, and the bosoms heaved, and the mascara ran, and the tears fell upon the beglittered gathering like rain leaking down a crystal chandelier. And Mister Rogers finally looked up from his watch and said softly, 'May God be with you,' to all his vanquished children."[12]

No one ever heard Mr. Rogers raise his voice. He always told the truth. He loved children. He exercised gentleness and love. That's a legacy. Sounds like a great hero and role model for kids — even if it was another generation. But he was just a man, and as kids age, they'll outgrow their need for ones like him.

But it's safe to say Mr. Rogers was well acquainted with someone else who loved to gather little children around him — someone who is a man's man, an awesome Father, a gentle Teacher, a faithful Son, a wonderful Friend. He is good, kind, meek, and consistent; he is a precious healer with a heart as big as heaven, someone for whom kids will never outgrow their need. And to every person, and especially to every mom and child, he says, "You're special."

If you as a mom want a perfect role model for your child, you won't have to look any further for a "nurturing place" than the pages of God's Word. There you'll see Jesus, lover of children — and adults — again and again saying, "Come to me. I'm everything you need."

Jesus is not just a legacy. He is the *real* model. And he is life itself. Introduce him to your kids early.

DAY-BREAK

Who are your children's role models? How are you introducing them to Jesus, the real model?

DAY-BRIEF

Heroes never really die — in our memories or in our hearts.

DAY-VOTEDLY YOURS

Lord Jesus, you are my only real role model. Help me to teach my children to love you, honor you, and live for you all the days of their lives.

day 36
king's kids

*For the jar of flour was not used up and the jug of oil
did not run dry, in keeping with the word
of the LORD spoken by Elijah.*
1 Kings 17:16

The widow was gathering sticks to build a fire and cook one last meal for her and her son when the prophet Elijah asked for a drink. A famine had ravaged the land, and God had been feeding the prophet Elijah in miraculous ways. But as the woman turned with her son to find the prophet some water, he made a second request: "And bring me, please, a piece of bread" (1 Kings 17:11).

She objected at first, explaining she only had enough for two. The prophet insisted that she bake all three of them some bread and promised her that God would provide a constant supply of oil and flour for her if she obeyed.

The woman could have refused and in anger replied, "Are you kidding? This is all we have. Where is God in all this? He has taken away everything! What use is it to go on living?" Her son could have heard her and become fearful, withdrawn, and anxious. But though she felt desperation, she acted in faith. I'm sure her willing attitude helped lighten her son's fear of imminent death too (1 Kings 17:7 – 16).

That biblical story reminded me of one I heard years ago about a young mother whose family was going through hard times. Her husband had lost his job, and they had three children to support. She had stretched their dollars as much as possible, but she knew things looked hopeless. When she looked in the pantry one day, she saw that it was almost completely bare. Even their dog knew there were no bones to spare.

The mother thought about what she should say to her family as they gathered around the empty table at dinnertime that evening, and how it would make her husband feel. He was trying hard to find work, but nothing had panned out. She didn't want to make him feel inadequate or her children anxious. *What would my mom do?* Suddenly she had an idea.

She took a single box of Jell-O and found just enough ingredients remaining on the shelves to make a few biscuits. The mother worked quickly and set the table in her best china, tablecloth, and silverware. She was glad they hadn't resorted to selling these yet, because they were wedding gifts from her late mom.

When the kids came home from school, they saw the fancy table settings and said, "Mom, who's coming to dinner tonight?"

"Some very special guests. It's a surprise. Be sure to clean up before dinner and dress especially nice for company."

Her husband asked the same question when he returned home from job-hunting, and she repeated the same instructions. She refused to add any more details.

Later that evening, she called everyone to dinner. They gathered around and said, "Where's the company? You said we were having special guests tonight."

The mom gathered her prepared food and laid it on the table. She smiled and replied, "You! All of *you* are my special guests. And I have prepared a fabulous feast of biscuits and Jell-O, fit for kings and queens, especially for you! Come and enjoy!"

No one dared to argue with Mom that evening. Dad eventually found work, and life returned to some normalcy. To this day, the kids still talk about the memory of Mom, years ago, standing in her Sunday best like a queen waving her magic wand — and their feast of biscuits and Jell-O.

No one is exempt from situations like the biblical widow or the modern-day mom. Because of America's financial situation at the writing of these day-votions, moms share a new fear for their families. Not only are some of their pantries bare; they no longer own homes in which to fill them. The *Dallas Morning News* reported that "Dallas-area school districts are seeing more homeless children this year … a nationwide trend spawned by families losing their jobs, their houses — and struggling just to pay bills."[13] The paper reported that even middle-class homeowners are renting or moving in with in-laws.

> *Modeling before our families that we are children of a King and not paupers will affect our kids for life.*

Whether we are the ones facing those difficult situations or simply feeling the financial pinch other ways as we try to stretch our resources as never before, we moms can make a difference with our attitudes. Modeling before our families that we are children of a King and not paupers will affect them for life. Do *you* believe in a God who will ultimately "meet all your needs according to the riches of his glory in Christ Jesus?" (Philippians 4:19) (even if it means in a temporary homeless shelter)? There's a good chance if you don't, your kids won't either.

The King of kings is not a stingy God, and he has resources we don't even know about. Whether it's biscuits and Jell-O or oil and flour, he wants us to trust him. Even in poverty "the cheerful heart has a continual feast" (Proverbs 15:15).

As a grateful, trusting mom, you may be the key to helping your children feel — and act — like "King's kids."

DAY-BREAK

Has your family ever had to endure a financial crisis? How did you handle it? How has God been faithful to you in the midst of those circumstances, and what did he teach you through them?

DAY-BRIEF

A good attitude is the key that unlocks many doors.

DAY-VOTEDLY YOURS

Father, you have never let my family or me starve. I trust you to provide exactly what we need, even in the hardest of times. Your love is my greatest feast. Forgive me when my faith falters, and help me to teach my children how blessed we really are.

when the new mom comes to town

Love is patient, love is kind … It always protects, always trusts, always hopes, always perseveres. Love never fails.
1 Corinthians 13:4, 7 – 8

When Sarah Wheaton, a single woman, answers a newspaper advertisement as a mail-order bride for Jacob Witting, a Kansas widower with two children, she faces the challenge of leaving her beloved Maine. Sarah misses the "colors of the sea" from her home so much that the children fear she will abandon them when she makes a trip to town.

The children need a mother, but can the wispy New Englander in the award-winning novel and Hallmark movie *Sarah, Plain and Tall* replace the sadness and memories still lodged in the family's hearts about their mom who died? And can the new family replace the longing Sarah feels for her place back home? Jacob only wants a woman who will "make a difference" with his kids. But Sarah does much more than that.

In the end, Sarah's trip to town ended not in a train trip back to Maine, but in a purchase of blue, green, and gray colored pencils for the children. She brought the "colors of the sea" to them. She succeeded in winning the hearts of the children — and Jacob.

That's Hollywood, you say, not real life. But as a mom, you may be facing the same dilemmas, or you know someone who is. What happens when death interrupts a family and a new mom comes to town? You may not look or act like their former, beloved caregiver. The kids may refuse to budge, feeling insecure and loyal to the only mom they've ever known. How can you make it a win/win situation, especially when your worlds are so far apart?

One thing's for sure. You can't force love, loyalty, or affection. Give time for God to paint his beauty and the "colors of the sea" in the lives of those children. Accusations like, "You're not my mom! I don't have to!" can sting. The kids may be testing you to see how long you'll stay. Will you "leave," like their late mom? Fear of abandonment can erupt all over again.

Soft and gentle replies may not win kids' hearts instantly, but when you refuse to retaliate and work together patiently as a couple, you'll narrow the distance between the "New England sea" and the "Kansas prairie." The familiar truth that "one of the best gifts a parent can give their children is a mom and dad who love each other" needs to find a new home in your children's hearts again.

> *God can bridge the gap between new mom*
> *and child and bring rich colors of the sea*
> *into your barren prairies.*

If you are blending two sets of kids as a result of divorce or remarriage after your husband's death, they all need evidence to restore their belief that "love never fails" (1 Corinthians 13:8).

What about when you're grown and a mother yourself, and a new mom enters the picture, marrying your aging father? Or when your adopted child's birth mother suddenly calls you and says she'd like to be part of her child's life again somehow? After all, you've been the only "real" mom your child has ever known. Are the emotions any less difficult?

No one can truly replace a mom at any age. Like Sarah Wheaton wisely did, the new mom can help preserve the child's former memories and attachments to their real mom while trying simply to love and to make a difference.

Whether you're a "Sarah, plain and tall" or a "Bertha, short and plump" (fictitious name, I assure you), God can bridge the gap between new mom and child and bring rich colors of the sea into your barren prairies. Your adjustment won't be easy, and you will wonder at times if it's worth the work. Love no matter what, and remember that while we are human and frail, God's love truly never fails. He will never abandon his children.

And that includes you as a mom.

DAY-BREAK

If you are the "new mom," how have you handled the challenges of your role? How can you encourage someone else who may be going through some "prairie" adjustments?

DAY-BRIEF

Love is the most beautiful color of all.

DAY-VOTEDLY YOURS

Lord, thank you that no matter what I experience as a mom, you never abandon me. You are there beside me, carrying me, walking with me, or holding my hand. Paint colors of beauty in my children's lives, and help them to believe in your love that never fails.

day 38
a higher calling

And we know that in all things God works for the good
of those who love him, who have been called
according to his purpose.
Romans 8:28

I could still visualize his youthful smile and innocent eyes. A large array of flowers adorned the front of the church and the closed casket, where a framed picture of a happy youth stood out in contrast to the silver-gray box.

My thoughts ran rampant as I rehearsed the shocking events of the last few days: a truck, a new motorcycle, a teenage boy and his Bible, and a family who had already endured tragedy numerous times.

Lowell was so young, and he seemed so different from the other youth in our church. In a crowd of young people, he always stood out. Barely sixteen, he was full of life. He was known as the kid who always took his Bible to school and who never apologized for the faith he represented so well. His death seemed so … senseless.

Elizabeth knew what it was like to bear a child who was different. God told her husband Zechariah early on that this child, born to them in their advanced years, "will be a joy and delight to you, and many will rejoice because of his birth, for he will be great in the sight of the Lord ... And he will go on before the Lord, in the spirit and power of Elijah, to turn the hearts of the parents to their children ... to make ready a people prepared for the Lord" (Luke 1:14 – 17).

John the Baptist was indeed different — a wild-looking man who lived in the desert, garbed himself in camel's hair clothing, and fed on locusts and wild honey (Mark 1:6). His ministry was short-lived, probably no more than a couple of years. Did Elizabeth know that her son's life would end in such a senseless death — in his beheading at the whim of a vengeful king's wife (Mark 6:14 – 29)? Was she even alive to witness his tragic end? Scripture doesn't say, but she did understand he was born for a mission: to prepare the way of the Lord. Even the prophets of old had talked about him. His life and purpose were indeed unique.

Though their individual "missions" cannot possibly be compared equally — an ordinary youth and Jesus' own cousin — Lowell and John both lived for a higher calling, and both exchanged their short, temporary residence for a heavenly home that would last forever.

Some of you know what it's like to lose a child, whether a baby, a child, a youth, or a young adult. And although you might not label your child "different," in the sense that they were not unusually gifted and had no exceptional "mission," you would no doubt still call them special gifts of God. All children are. Their deaths may not have seemed as senseless as Lowell's or John the Baptist's, or as the kids who were killed in the Columbine or Virginia Tech tragedies, but does death ever make sense to a mom?

When your children are old enough,
one of the strongest messages you can instill
in their lives is that they were born for a
higher calling than just to live and die.

When your children are old enough, one of the strongest messages you can instill in their lives is that they were born for a higher calling than just to live and die. They may not wear camel's hair, but we can clothe them in the armor of God: a belt of truth, a breastplate of righteousness, the helmet of salvation, shoes of peace, and the sword of the Spirit (God's Word) (Ephesians 6:14 – 17). And they may not eat weird food, but we can show them where to find their daily bread. They may not live in the desert, but we can teach them where "home" really is — heaven.

My child was barely formed when I lost our first baby through miscarriage. That doesn't compare to losing an older child, but questions still came. While we may never understand God's purposes for what seems like a premature death, we can be sure of God's dual "higher calling," whether we've ever lost a child or not. One is that every child is called to prepare the way for Jesus in another's heart — to live for him.

The other "high" calling is for us as moms. We share the same one as our kids, but in addition, God uses us to help prepare the soil in our own children's hearts so they can better understand God's universal calling for their lives. They may reject our teaching, but our calling remains, regardless.

Should death rip away our most precious gifts, we may look for clear answers and complete understanding. But we probably won't find them. Not now, and maybe not until we finally arrive at our new "home." God doesn't expect us to. What he does want us to understand is that we live in an imperfect world, but he is a perfect God — filled with compassion, comfort, and hope. He hurts with us! Jesus too experienced what *seemed* like a cruel, senseless, premature death. Our kids are all great in his sight, and he loves them all equally. He wants to remind us that our home here on earth is truly temporary.

But he is also a God who promises that all things — in life or death — will work together for his good purposes. Trusting him for that truth is probably one of the highest callings — and most difficult of all.

In time, God will allow us to comfort others because of the way he has comforted us (2 Corinthians 1:3 – 4). When that happens, God gives us a tiny glimpse into the good that he can bring out of an otherwise seemingly unredeemable situation. That's part of what makes the body of Christ strong, when they join together in that higher calling and share together each other's joys and sorrows.

DAY-BREAK

Have you ever lost a child? What sustained you through that loss? Has someone close to you gone through that tragedy? Pray for those you know who have. Refrain from dispensing pat answers; instead, give them a hug each time you see them and offer to help practically any way you can.

DAY-BRIEF

For believers, death is not the end, but the beginning of life.

DAY-VOTEDLY YOURS

God, thank you for being a compassionate God and for your comfort in times of sorrow. Help me to teach my children how to live for Jesus as their mission and with heaven on their mind.

day 39
switched at birth

If any of you lacks wisdom, you should ask God,
who gives generously to all ... and it will be given to you.
But when you ask, you must believe and not doubt.
James 1:5 – 6

Two new mothers came to King Solomon's court, pleading for an answer to their dilemma. Soon after birth, one of their babies died during the night, probably from suffocation. That baby's mother crept into the other woman's room and took her living infant, leaving the still body of her own child in the other woman's bed. When the mother woke up, she discovered her baby had been switched, and the dead child left in its place.

She found the mom who made the switch, and a verbal fight followed, ending up with a visit to the king for his decision. The guilty mom would not own up to the truth (1 Kings 3:16 – 23).

God had given King Solomon a choice when he first took the throne: he could ask God for anything he wanted, and God would grant it. But rather than offering selfish requests, Solomon asked for wisdom. God gave him that and so much more. The women's arguments would test that gift of wisdom (1 Kings 3:4 – 14).

King Solomon listened to the women's accusations, then made his decision: "Cut the living child in two and give half to one and half to the other" (1 Kings 3:25). Wise king!

Sure enough, the real mother was horrified and offered to give up the baby rather than see him die. The guilty mom could care less. Her heartless response may seem unbelievable to us: "Neither I nor you shall have him. Cut him in two!" (1 Kings 3:26).

Solomon knew the real mother would speak up, so he promptly awarded the baby to its mother.

Some of you may feel like your child must have been switched at birth, especially when they challenge your authority or decisions. Every mother needs a healthy dose of wisdom when it comes time to answer the inevitable questions: How long should you breast-feed your baby? Will you allow one, two, or multiple body piercing (the ears being only one of the choices)? Can they date at sixteen or twenty-five? Will you follow them on their dates or just hire a private investigator? Will you send them to their rooms or take away their driver's license? Will you let them live at home free or make them pay rent?

> **When we ask, God gives generously,
> but he wants us to act like real mothers of faith
> and believe that God will do what he says.**

Moms could ask God for many things: a compliant, obedient child, one who hates sports (to save money on hospital bills), maybe even a valedictorian (to ensure a paid college scholarship). And you might just give birth to one of those.

However, real life always includes challenges. Not every decision will have a clear-cut, black-and-white answer, like the one above with the two moms. The best decision a mom can make is to ask God for wisdom, just as King Solomon did. The Bible says it's better than asking for money: "How much better to get wisdom than gold, to get insight rather than silver!" (Proverbs 16:16). Wisdom helps build a successful home: "By wisdom a house is built, and through understanding it is established; through knowledge its rooms are filled with rare and beautiful treasures" (Proverbs 24:3 – 4). And wisdom is an effective tool in heated arguments: "Wisdom is better than weapons of war" (Ecclesiastes 9:18).

When we ask, God gives generously, but he wants us to act like real mothers of faith and believe that God will do what he says. The next time it's crucial decision-making time, you may hear a divine whisper in your spirit. God may be allowing a heavy test of your gift when you hear him saying, "Will the real mom please speak up?"

Rest assured, when you use his Word as your authority and his love as your motivation, you will usually make the right decision.

DAY-BREAK

What kinds of decisions as a mom have been hardest for you? How has God given you wisdom in some trying situations? What would you do differently next time?

DAY-BRIEF

Ask not what God can do for you. Ask God what you can do for him.

DAY-VOTEDLY YOURS

God, how desperately I need your wisdom as a mom! Give me a discerning heart so I can face every decision that comes. Make me the kind of mother who knows how to point her children in the right direction — to your love.

beauty in the midst

One thing I ask from the LORD,
  this only do I seek:
that I may dwell in the house of the LORD
  all the days of my life,
to gaze on the beauty of the LORD.

Psalm 27:4

Most retail businesses require a year-end inventory of their merchandise. It helps them determine future orders and helps measure past progress. *Hmm. Maybe moms should take an inventory. It has been a few years …*

That sounds like a good idea, harmless enough, don't you think? So you schedule some time for your inventory. Maybe you decide to do a walk-through in your home for starters. But as you turn the corner, you happen to pass by the full-length mirror. One glance reminds you that Barbie doesn't live here anymore (did she ever?). Exercise consists of either chasing the kids through the house or racing to the car to get to work on time. You did serve some low-cal, takeout food on your Royal China last week. Does that count?

Motherhood may have left its mark on you. *Maybe if I change the color of my hair,* you think out loud, as if that would hide the, um, bulges you notice. *Maybe it's the mirror.*

Your inventory has only started, but you're feeling anything but encouraged. As you continue, you shake your head. *So much for personal appearance. I'll just inventory the house.*

In reality, a quick stroll through your house gives evidence that Cinderella's fella never found her slipper. The carriage must have turned back into a pumpkin, and it looks like something bigger than mice have invaded every room in your house.

As you look around, you realize your kids don't understand that mud belongs in the yard, along with big dogs and pet frogs. You wonder if placing a "Condemned" sign on your kids' doors would help.

You enter the kids' bathroom, then quickly close the door and exit. Maybe the kitchen's in better shape. So you check out the pantry and refrigerator and realize you need to stop. *Who thought up this inventory anyway? Bad idea!*

We moms might not conduct an actual year-end inventory, but all of us second-guess ourselves repeatedly. In front of you is your imaginary list, and you mentally rehearse it: Proverbs woman? *Nope.* Supermom? *Not hardly.* Organized? *I wish.* Decorator? *Not creative enough.* Gourmet chef? *Ha!* Beautiful? *No way.* Good manager of time? *Not usually.* Wait. Stop. You're on a fast track to depression.

> *Thank God for the beauty*
> *— and fragrance — he is creating in the lives*
> *of your family members, including you.*

Running a household requires time, work, and energy — and

delegation. Too many moms live by the "If it's going to be, it's up to me" philosophy. Don't be afraid to ask for help. *Busy* can easily become a badge we wear to stoke our own self-esteem. *Am I the only one who gives a flip around here? I have obligations too, you know!* Yet we don't form a plan, assign tasks, or require follow-through.

Moms may have to adjust expectations for their kids and their homes (and themselves) during these years when kids are shuttling in and out, but they can still work together as a family. Unless you're single, ask your husband to help you with solutions. Together, you can make a great team. Remember that relationships matter more than fussing over a messy house. Create order where you can, but let perfection go.

In time your home will empty. So will the mess. But in the meantime, is there anything you can do to restore order, beauty, and simplicity in the midst of the chaotic years — and in the lives of your family?

Exchange old thinking patterns to an "If it's going to be, it's up to thee" philosophy. Then start with a sweet-smelling flower. Every place you see a "mess," place a flower in the midst of the chaos to remind you that beauty still lives there: on the bathroom cabinet, on your home office desk, near the kitchen sink, in your kid's room. Each time you look at that flower, thank God for the beauty — and fragrance — he is creating in the lives of your family members, including you. Place your favorite Bible verse next to the flower vase. Think of your house as God's home.

Make it your goal to work on only one area of your life and your home at a time. Establishing one good habit (like exercise, for example) may help make other disciplines a little easier.

Remember that God doesn't look at our outward appearance; he looks at the heart (1 Samuel 16:7). At the same time, we — and our homes — are a reflection of the beauty of Christ (2 Corinthians 3:18). Ask him to show you the balance between those two truths. Then meet him in the middle.

When we focus on God and his beauty, he can turn our messes into mists of fragrance that sweeten up everyone — and every room — in our homes.

DAY-BREAK

If you were to take an inventory of your home and your life as a mom, how would it read? What disciplines would you like to see improve? What can you do to help focus on God's beauty more?

DAY-BRIEF

Where there is love in the heart, there is beauty in the home.

DAY-VOTEDLY YOURS

Lord, where you are, there is always beauty. In the midst of my messes, I will focus on you and on the fragrance you are creating in the lives of my family.

epilogue

Perhaps you have never come to know and enjoy the intimate presence of God personally. If he has placed such a desire in your heart, may I share with you some simple steps so you can become acquainted with him and become a child of God forever?

1. Admit the sin in your life and the need in your heart for God (see Romans 3:23).
2. Acknowledge that Jesus loves you and that he died for your sin (see John 3:16).
3. Recognize his salvation is a gift, not something earned (see Romans 6:23; Ephesians 2:8 – 9).
4. Ask Jesus to forgive you, to come into your life, and to fill you with his personal, intimate presence (John 1:12).
5. By faith, thank him that you are now God's child, and confess that from now on, he will be the Lord and Love of your life. Give Jesus the keys to all the rooms of your heart (see Romans 10:9 – 10).

If this book has encouraged you, I'd love to hear from you. And if I can help you in your Christian growth in any way, please let me know. For more information, see my websites: www.rebeccabarlowjordan.com or www.day-votions.com.

Rebecca Barlow Jordan

notes

1. Rebecca Barlow Jordan, © DaySpring Cards, Used by permission.
2. Chip Ingram, "The Miracle of Life Change," *Masterworks* (Nashville: Lifeway, Winter 2008 – 2009), 13.
3. Todd J. Gillman, "Mindful of Imperiled Legacy, Bush Addresses A&M Grads," *The Dallas Morning News*, Section 1A, 4A, Saturday, December 13, 2008.
4. *NIV Archaeological Study Bible* (Grand Rapids: Zondervan, 2005), 279, 983.
5. Kenneth L. Price, *The Eagle Christian* (Montgomery, Ala.: Old Faithful Press, 1984).
6. *Seventh Heaven*, season 11, episode 16: "Gimme That Ol' Time Religion," TV.com, Seventh Heaven: Episode Guide (February 11, 2007), www.tv.com/7th-heaven/show251/episode.html (February 17, 2009).
7. Kyle Dodd, Family Life Conference, Weekend to Remember, February 14, 2009.
8. Jill Savage, *Is There Really Sex after Kids?* (Grand Rapids: Zondervan, 2003), 13.
9. Ibid., 177.
10. Steve Harman, "On Elephant Sanctuary: Unlikely Friends," January 2, 2009, *CBS Evening News*: www.cbsnews.com/stories/2009/01/02/assignment_america/main4696340.shtml (accessed March 5, 2009).
11. "Fred Rogers," Wikipedia, the free encyclopedia, Last modified

March 7, 2009, en.wikipedia.org/wiki/Fred_Rogers (accessed March 7, 2009).

12. Ibid.

13. Stella M. Chavez, "Number of Homeless Students on the Rise," *Dallas Morning News*, Section 1B, Sunday, March 1, 2009.

DAY-VOTIONS®
Rebecca Barlow Jordan

**Day-votions® for
Grandmothers:** Heart to
Heart Encouragement

**Day-votions® for
Women:** Heart to Heart
Encouragement

**Day-votions® for
Mothers:** Heart to Heart
Encouragement

Introducing a new series of Day-votions® from bestselling inspirational author Rebecca Barlow Jordan. This beautiful, lighthearted series of devotional books is perfect for you and is a perfect gift for women of all seasons, and all stages of life.

Available in stores and online!

Share Your Thoughts

With the Author: Your comments will be forwarded to the author when you send them to *zauthor@zondervan.com*.

With Zondervan: Submit your review of this book by writing to *zreview@zondervan.com*.

Free Online Resources at
www.zondervan.com

Zondervan AuthorTracker: Be notified whenever your favorite authors publish new books, go on tour, or post an update about what's happening in their lives at www.zondervan.com/authortracker.

Daily Bible Verses and Devotions: Enrich your life with daily Bible verses or devotions that help you start every morning focused on God. Visit www.zondervan.com/newsletters.

Free Email Publications: Sign up for newsletters on Christian living, academic resources, church ministry, fiction, children's resources, and more. Visit www.zondervan.com/newsletters.

Zondervan Bible Search: Find and compare Bible passages in a variety of translations at www.zondervanbiblesearch.com.

Other Benefits: Register yourself to receive online benefits like coupons and special offers, or to participate in research.